Three
PRAYERS

THE THREE MOST POWERFUL PRAYERS
THAT EVERY CHRISTIAN SHOULD BE PRAYING

ROBERT NORTH

BALBOA.
PRESS

A DIVISION OF HAY HOUSE

Balboa Press books may be ordered through booksellers or by contacting:

Balboa Press
A Division of Hay House
1663 Liberty Drive
Bloomington, IN 47403
www.balboapress.com
1 (877) 407-4847

Because of the dynamic nature of the Internet, any web addresses or links contained in this book may have changed since publication and may no longer be valid. The views expressed in this work are solely those of the author and do not necessarily reflect the views of the publisher, and the publisher hereby disclaims any responsibility for them.

The author of this book does not dispense medical advice or prescribe the use of any technique as a form of treatment for physical, emotional, or medical problems without the advice of a physician, either directly or indirectly. The intent of the author is only to offer information of a general nature to help you in your quest for emotional and spiritual well-being. In the event you use any of the information in this book for yourself, which is your constitutional right, the author and the publisher assume no responsibility for your actions.

Any people depicted in stock imagery provided by Thinkstock are models, and such images are being used for illustrative purposes only.
Certain stock imagery © Thinkstock.

Print information available on the last page.

ISBN: 978-1-5043-5582-7 (sc)
ISBN: 978-1-5043-5584-1 (hc)
ISBN: 978-1-5043-5583-4 (e)

Library of Congress Control Number: 2016906355

Balboa Press rev. date: 08/09/2016

Baker's Evangelical Dictionary of Biblical Theology references remembrance as that "which points to making present the past, so that it can be effective in the present." Printed by permission of Baker Publishing Group.

I would like to thank Joan Hunter of Joan Hunter Ministries for allowing me to include a prayer that she teaches. It is an extraordinary prayer of forgiveness that provides freedom from spiritual bondage. I have incorporated this prayer within the Communion Prayer. Joan Hunter has a powerful prayer ministry. If you wish to learn more of her ministry, visit joanhunter.org.

I wish to thank Dr. Win Wachsmann for permission to share some of his documented military miracles. He has recorded several amazing miracles. Visit Militarymiracles.com

I wish to thank Jill Boyce the "Bandana Lady" for permission to share of military miracles that occurred during Operation Iraqi Freedom. Her ministry to our soldiers in the armed forces provides an open door for miraculous intervention. If you wish to learn more of her ministry visit: thePsalm91bandana.com.

Special Acknowledgment

I would like to especially thank my mother for her encouragement and support. She has been supportive in my endeavors to finish this work.

CONTENTS

INTRODUCTION

THE PURPOSE OF PRAYER

A time of tribulation unprecedented in the history of mankind is rapidly approaching. Judgments of every kind are exhibited everywhere—and the followers of Jesus Christ do not know what to do.

It is for this reason that the Lord has encouraged me to share with my Christian brothers and sisters the following revelations that will help prepare us for the immediate future and beyond.

Revelation on the following three prayers is provided for the express purpose of learning how to escape many of the brutal judgments that are coming upon this sin-laden world.

There is a *means of escape.*

There is a *place of safety.*

There is a *powerful means of deliverance.*

Appropriating a means of escape, a place of safety, and deliverance from evil for ourselves will depend on how resourceful and diligent we are for preparing for our future *now.*

By activating the following prayers, we can secure a more excellent future. Through prayer, we can alter and change events forthcoming in our life. We can be spared much agony if we learn what and how to pray for ourselves. But knowledge in itself is not enough; we have to actually put it into practice and establish a meaningful prayer life, and we must develop a prayer life that is effective. If we implement a prayer life now, we can and will be spared much unnecessary agony and grief.

It is my prayer and wish that many will discover and receive the protection of the Lord during these difficult times. The Lord's hand is not short that He cannot deliver and provide safety.

The prayers found in this book are basic, in that they provide everything we need. But it is up to us to activate the Word of God in our lives so that the Lord may intervene in our behalf.

May the blessings of the Lord be fulfilled within us all.

—Robert North

CHAPTER 1

MAKE ME "RAPTURE-READY": A PRAYER GUIDE

One day while I was in prayer, the Lord showed me three prayers that are crucial for the preparation and survival of Christians in these last days. The Lord revealed the value of these prayers and how they will play a vital role in our preservation. They will provide deliverance from many destructive situations. They will provide us peace and protection as we encounter persecution and hardships of every kind. They will open wide a door into the miraculous, and we will see many angelic interventions unprecedented in the history of mankind.

We do not have to be overwhelmed with fear or hopelessness. We can alter our destinies. As judgments are poured out upon all of mankind, we can be powerful witnesses to the saving grace of God's mighty hand of intervention.

As we secure our positions through prayer, two incredible situations will occur. The first situation will be an opportunity to witness to those who will seek to know this God who has provided miraculously on our behalf. There will be a great opportunity for evangelism, and we must be prepared for this.

The second situation will be severe persecution. Many ungodly people in the world will harden their hearts and express their hatred toward us. One of the most unexpected sources of persecution will not come from outside the church but from within the church. Christians who have neither surrendered their lives to Jesus Christ nor established any kind of a personal relationship with Jesus will hate us. God will not intervene on their behalf as He will for us. Jealousy will flood their hearts with hatred, just as it did with Cain before he slew his brother, Abel.

Christians who prepare themselves with prayer can place a mighty roadblock in front of rigid, religious Christians who may seek their demise.

Persecution will come, but there is a way to prepare ourselves, to protect ourselves, and to change the outcome and course of our futures.

The revelation I received of the Lord revealed how these prayers will establish a supernatural barrier of protection that will secure situations of safety and provide fearless peace in the midst of great turmoil and strife.

Christians will encounter several things before the rapture of the church. We Christians will become engaged in a battle for our own protection and safety on a scale unprecedented in history. Persecution will rage against true followers of Jesus Christ. Deliverance and safety will become major concerns. Faith, hope, and God's love will become essentials that must be rooted and grounded deep within our hearts.

Our hearts must become totally saturated with the very presence of God—the very presence of His glory. Our hearts must be secured with the power of His presence so that we may not be easily shaken or distressed, for our enemy, Satan, stands ready to unleash an attack upon mankind with situations of unspeakable despair and hopelessness.

As the wicked raise their voices of defiance and boldly challenge God's directives, we will find ourselves immersed in the midst of God's judgments. These are judgments that God will dispense upon the ungodly because of their own ungodly acts of rebellion.

Jesus Christ is able to provide in times of difficulty for those who follow Him. God has the ability to warn and to prepare or to remove us from destruction. With His miraculous hand of intervention, we can remain unscathed by any judgment that He sends upon the earth, and by His mighty hand, we can receive miraculous deliverance from any of Satan's efforts to destroy us. It is necessary that we become diligent in our efforts, spending time with the Lord Jesus Christ and *listening* to Him.

Remember the Israelites in Egypt. They sat right in the middle of every judgment and every plague God poured out upon the ungodly, and they were spared. They did not suffer any of the torments of the rebellious and defiant. They did, however, suffer ridicule, hatred, and ill treatment from those who were being judged.

Those who tormented the chosen of God were themselves grievously tormented. Many who brazenly opposed God continued to harden their hearts in defiance, and their hatred intensified until they became mad with revenge and rage. The Israelites *listened to God's instruction* for preservation, and they were kept safe. They were told to fill water pots with water before God turned water into blood. Warning was given beforehand to shelter their livestock and to take refuge from a deadly hailstorm. All of Israel was instructed to shelter behind blood-covered doorposts that would prevent death from entering their houses. Peace and safety followed those who obeyed God's instruction.

Simply being an Israelite did not offer protection. They had to be obedient to His instruction in order to be spared hardship, death, and destruction. They had to seek God, listen to what He said, and then act upon the instructions that were delivered.

Simply being a Christian will not offer you protection. Deliverance, protection, and safety will not automatically come to us because we are faithful in attending church or giving tithes or because we are involved in many good and charitable works. Though these things may help, they will not provide the protection we need.

Christians, we have to be in fellowship with the Lord Jesus Christ. We have to be able to hear His voice and His instruction.

We have to be obedient to what He reveals to us and take action in those things that He instructs us to do.

Jesus said, "My sheep know my voice." If we cannot hear His voice, how will we know what to do? If we cannot spend time in His presence, how can we learn His voice?

Christians are about to face a horrific battle. We will come face-to-face with persecution and ridicule. We will come face-to-face with situations of desperation for our basic needs. We will earnestly desire the Lord's protection from the elements of nature, from political unrest, from ruthless and violent actions of insanity, and from hatred and jealousy of those who are within the church, as well as from those who are without.

It will be hard to deal with hatred, offenses, and the absence of forgiveness. Food, clothing, and shelter will become matters of desperation. There is no better way to prepare for the future than to pray for a protected future. We must secure ourselves in the Lord *now*. The longer we delay, the more difficult it will become.

THREE PRAYERS

The three prayers presented in this book will prepare us for our future, create peace and safety, and provide deliverance and protection. Most important of all, they will make us "rapture-ready."

I was shown these three crucial prayers in these last days. It is very important that we implement these prayers in our *daily* prayer lives, beginning today. Establishing a prayer life—*a daily prayer life*—is the most important thing that we, as Christians, can do *now*. These prayers provide all that we will need for our survival—and we are now entering survival mode.

CHAPTER 2

PRAYER OF PROTECTION

The first prayer, which is Psalm 91, is a great prayer of protection and deliverance. It is also a powerful warfare psalm that any soldier of the Lord can use to defeat the enemies of disaster, death, disease, and destruction. It has proved itself over and over again.

This prayer has produced many miraculous results—many lives have been spared because of this prayer. It is definitely one to memorize.

The great revivalist John G Lake believed in the powerful promises of God's Word. During a great plague in South Africa he never suffered any ill effects. English doctors actually observed (under the microscope) the death of deadly bubonic germs when Lake would touch them with his hands.

Charles Spurgeon tells a story of a shoemaker in Germany who posted in his store window a hand written copy of Psalm

91:9-19. Though thousands perished in a great cholera plague - he, his family, and his customers were protected.

In 2003 Operation Iraqi Freedom there are numerous testimonies of supernatural intervention. There are testimonies of soldiers standing within the kill radius of mortar explosions that did not suffer any shrapnel or blast injuries.

There is one account of an enemy RPG rocket piercing a Humvee and exploding inside. Miraculously four soldiers emerged unaffected by the percussion of the blast.

There is another account of about a dozen AAV,s (military vehicles) forming a steel wall of protection and firing into the enemy. These phantom AAV's disappeared as quickly as they appeared. They were not of any known operations.

I also read that, more recently, a mother purchased special bandanas with Psalm 91 printed on them and gave them to her son and to everyone in his unit. This unit was deployed to Iraq during "Operation Iraqi Freedom" and was part of an extremely hazardous operation. Only 50 percent of the 150-man unit were expected to return home alive. However, despite all the mortar attacks, snipers, roadside bombs, and ambushes they endured for nearly a year, all 150 men returned home alive and well. These men made it a practice to recite Psalm 91 on a daily basis.

A greater realization of the importance of this prayer made me aware of the need to be protected from the violent acts of terrorism that will plague our country. When the Twin Towers went down, well over one hundred Christians were spared from death in a number of miraculous ways. Many of these Christians had paved a road of protection and deliverance through prayer.

While pondering the miraculous interventions of the prayer of Psalm 91 during my devotional time, I heard clearly in my spirit the gentle voice of the Lord. He said, "If you are fighting any kind of battle in your life, you need to pray this prayer daily."

My views on Psalm 91 took on a whole new dimension. Our daily combat with everyday life needs to be covered by prayer. This prayer covers every protection and deliverance needed in our daily lives.

As mentioned, the soldiers made it a practice to frequently recite Psalm 91. God is no respecter of persons. If He will intervene on their behalf, He will definitely intervene on our behalf—if we learn how to be consistent in our daily prayer lives.

There are numerous testimonies of miraculous interventions by individuals who have diligently prayed this prayer. Soldiers had the fortitude to pray this prayer daily. Will you?

Psalm 91

God's Great Prayer of Protection and Deliverance

He that dwelleth in the secret place of the most High shall abide under the shadow of the Almighty.

I will say of the Lord, He is my refuge and my fortress: my God; in him will I trust.

Surely he shall deliver thee from the snare of the fowler, and from the noisome pestilence.

He shall cover thee with his feathers, and under his wings shalt thou trust: his truth shall be thy shield and buckler.

Thou shalt not be afraid for the terror by night; nor for the arrow that flieth by day;

Nor for the pestilence that walketh in darkness; nor for the destruction that wasteth at noonday.

A thousand shall fall at thy side, and ten thousand at thy right hand; but it shall not come nigh thee.

Only with thine eyes shalt thou behold and see the reward of the wicked.

Because thou hast made the Lord, which is my refuge, even the most High, thy habitation;

There shall no evil befall thee, neither shall any plague come nigh thy dwelling.

For he shall give his angels charge over thee, to keep thee in all thy ways.

They shall bear thee up in their hands, lest thou dash thy foot against a stone.

Thou shalt tread upon the lion and adder: the young lion and the dragon shalt thou trample under feet.

Because he hath set his love upon me, therefore will I deliver him: I will set him on high, because he hath known my name.

He shall call upon me, and I will answer him: I will be with him in trouble; I will deliver him, and honour him.

With long life will I satisfy him, and shew him my salvation. (KJV)

CHAPTER 3

PRAYER OF TRANSFORMATION

We must learn how to pray for ourselves.

To learn that I was to be diligent in praying for myself was a new revelation for me. I had no idea that I could secure an entirely new personality and an entirely new transformation of my mind and heart through prayer. Even the desires of my heart could be transformed.

When I first was presented with this new concept of concentrated prayer for myself, I had some serious questions. And I asked the Lord to show me a validation in His Word of this new prayer principle. He showed me, "If any of you lack wisdom, let him ask of God, that giveth to all men liberally, and upbraideth not; and it shall be given him" (James 1:5 KJV).

"Do you want more of my wisdom than you have right now? Ask for it." He said if we want it, we can have it, but we *have to ask*! God will provide wisdom and revelation to us through daily fellowship with Him; this is normal. The problem, though, is that most Christians only spend five to fifteen minutes—at best— in their time of fellowship with the Lord. They will spend just enough time to "get by" on any given day.

When we only spend five to fifteen minutes a day, our relationship with the Lord will be severely limited. The Lord wants us to go beyond the normal daily revelations that we receive of Him. When we spend minimal time with the Lord, what we receive of Him will be minimal as well. We really cannot receive much of Him when we only allow Him a limited time frame each day.

Even so, if a short time is all we can afford to spend with the Lord, that is definitely better than not spending *any* time with the Lord at all. Those of us who desire to dwell in the deeper depths of His wisdom have to ask for it. We have to reach out and seek it. This *asking* forces us to make a determined effort. It is our responsibility to break the normal everyday confinement that limits our relationship with the Lord.

As I was pondering this new concept of praying for myself, new revelations began to flow through my mind. One interesting question presented itself in my spirit: *"Do you know why many of the prophets of old had a close relationship with Me?"* There was a pause. Then the answer came. *"It is because they knew how to pray for themselves."*

Immediately, I was shown Psalm 51:10. "Create in me a clean heart, O God; and renew a right spirit within me."

What did David pray for himself? He prayed for the creation of a clean heart and a right spirit. He prayed for the establishment of God's desires within his heart. He prayed for a transformation of his heart. He prayed for the Lord to replace the desires of his flesh with the Lord's desires for righteousness. He also prayed for the transformation of his own spirit.

All the sinful desires of the flesh can be replaced with God's desires for holiness and righteousness. We can pray for this incredible transformation of our hearts. We can trash our desires for sin and replace them with desires for righteousness through prayer.

The prophet David is not the only prophet to pray for the transformation of their own heart. Other prophets prayed many other personal prayers for themselves. The Lord was simply showing me that if I wanted a powerful supernatural experience with Him, I could pray for it.

If we want to be filled with the powerful presence of God and acquire an unmovable and secure relationship with the Lord that cannot be shaken, then we must pray for it.

"And to know the love of Christ, which passeth knowledge, that ye might be filled with all the fullness of God" (Ephesians 3:19 KJV).

How many of us know, by experience, the deeper depths of Christ's love that will allow us to be filled "with all the fullness of God"? How many of us can conceive of what it *really* means to be filled with the fullness of God?

It is *vitally important* that we realize that we can be filled with a much greater presence of God and His power. We can have a relationship with the Lord so secure that nothing can separate us from God. This is important because a powerful, "supernatural" tidal wave of doubt and deception will soon sweep the earth in a major effort to question the very existence of God. A flood of deception that will deny Jesus Christ and God has already begun, but this new wave will be fortified with supernatural power from our enemy, Satan. Do not ever underestimate the deceptive abilities of which he is capable. Believe me; he is far more intelligent than we possibly could imagine.

We are mere mortals. We do not even come close to the level of intelligence that demons have. The one thing that we have going for us, though, is the presence and the power of God that resides within us and through us. This is how we are able to overcome everything, including every demonic influence.

It is very important that we secure our relationship with the Lord Jesus Christ. We must never allow ourselves to be pushed into a corner of insecurity that would cause us to doubt or even deny the Lord.

CHAPTER 4

THE GREAT FALLING AWAY

Just prior to the rapture of the church, there will be a great persecution—a great falling away. Many who believe in Jesus Christ and have accepted Him as their Savior will turn away.

2 Thessalonians 2:3

"Let no one deceive or beguile you in any way, for that day will not come except the apostasy comes first [*unless the predicted great falling away of those who have professed to be Christians has come*], and the man of lawlessness (sin) is revealed, who is the son of doom (of perdition)," ... (AMP, emphasis added). [another reference is found in 1 Timothy 4:1.]

The following three primary events will cause many to become disillusioned, discouraged, and disgusted with the gospel of Christ:

1. Religious con artists—men who are in it for the social status, the glory, the limelight, and the money. Religious men may demonstrate supernatural powers but have no fruit of the Holy Spirit within them.
2. Doctrinal error and doctrines of demons will confuse, frustrate, and lead many from a personal relationship with the Lord.
3. Persecution. Many will not be able to withstand the pressures of persecution and rejection from the ungodly.

The abovementioned three events, in turn, will cause five major changes in the heart—five conditions of the heart that will destroy many Christians and cause them to fall away.

First, many will distance themselves from the Lord and lose the love that they had for the Lord. Their hearts will become cold and unresponsive to the Word of God and His love.

Leaving their first love will be the primary reason for the great falling away. When their love for the Lord Jesus Christ dwindles, they will allow the floodgates of fear, hatred, deception and unforgiveness to overwhelm them.

It will be easy to distance themselves from their prayer closets and the reading of God's Word. Things of the world will slowly creep into their daily activities and will replace their personal time with the Lord. Their confidence in their relationship with the Lord will diminish and allow doubt and faithlessness to flood their hearts. Guilt and condemnation will slowly overwhelm them with hopelessness. Despair will fill their hearts with fear. All of this will begin in very subtle ways.

Fear of persecution, of confrontation, of despairing situations, of being abandoned by God—these things create a heart full of desperation. Many will fall into error and horrible traps because of making bad decisions. It is simple: desperate people will do desperate things. And that includes many Christians.

Overwhelming feelings of rejection, unworthiness, and abandonment of God in their lives tends to cause them to run *from* God, rather than run *to* Him. It makes no difference if they were good Christians in the past. A failed relationship with the Lord will make them fearful and desperate.

Trusted friends, fellow Christians, and religious leaders will turn on these people in an instant in order to secure their own safety and preservation. They will be deliberately betrayed by many and unintentionally betrayed by a few. Failure to run to the Lord will allow their hearts to turn cold, lifeless, and hard.

It will become very difficult to forgive betrayal and rejection. Bitterness will act like a noose around their necks, except it will be around their hearts. It will cut off the air they breathe; it will prevent God's breath of life from restoring their hearts.

The most cunning and subtle of false and deceptive doctrines will mislead many and cause them to accept doctrines of demons and doctrines of permissive sins; these will actually alienate many from God. Through deceptive logic and subtle persuasive enticements, it will be easy to unknowingly create hearts that are defiant to God's Word and will. False doctrines always have a way of creating a rebellious heart toward God.

The only way to survive these last days of great turmoil is to establish our hearts in the deepest love relationship that we can with the Lord. We must protect ourselves from losing our love for God. We must not allow ourselves to be swallowed up in fear, overwhelmed with hatred, or to reject God's grace through deception. We need to start preparing and protecting our hearts right now.

"Keep thy heart with all diligence; for out of it are the issues of life" (Proverbs 4:23 KJV).

Proverbs 4:23 proclaims the importance of guarding our hearts as a major concern in our lives. It is also concerned with the "state of being" that the heart has obtained.

To remain steadfast and true, we need a heart that is transformed with the very character and nature of God.

We need a personal, secure relationship with Jesus Christ. And we need hearts that are firmly founded in the Word of God, that we may not be deceived in following another gospel that is false and misleading.

We need transformed hearts—we can pray for that. We can pray for our own hearts' conditions.

CHAPTER 5

DISCOVERING THE DESIRES OF GOD'S HEART

One afternoon, while talking with the Lord, He gave me instruction to take paper and a pen and sit down. He asked me two questions. The first was, "If *you* could have anything from Me that your heart desires, what would you ask for?" He had me make out a list of my desires. Anything I could ask Him for was to be written down. I wrote down everything that I could think of for myself, for family, for friends, and for anyone else I could think of. I covered every spiritual, mental, physical, material, financial, and social aspect. My list was extensive and big.

By asking this first question, I realized later that this was an ingenious way of getting the things of my flesh out of the way first. It paved the way for His next question.

The second question He asked also required the making of a list: "If *I* could have anything from you that *I* wanted, what would *I* ask for?"

Wow! Double wow! This was a major wake-up call. I didn't have to think long about His first desire on His list. I knew the first one. The first and greatest commandment above all commandments is Mark 12:30: "And thou shalt love the Lord thy God with all thy heart, and with all thy soul, and with all thy mind, and with all thy strength: this is the first commandment" (KJV).

What He wants more than anything else in all of heaven and earth is to be loved. He wants us to know Him with a profound intimacy that comes through the development of a close and personal relationship with Him. He wants to be loved by us— that's number one.

As I began to think of other things that He might desire of me, I realized that I was going to get myself into trouble if I tried to guess the other things on His list. So I asked Him to reveal the rest of His list to me. The following is seven desires that rank as the top seven on His list. He wanted me to be filled with

1. His love,
2. His righteousness,
3. His wisdom and revelation,
4. His peace
5. His joy,

6. the Holy Spirit, and

7. His blood.

The last one—being filled with His blood—was new to me. I had never heard of this before. When I inquired of the Lord about this, He showed me that I was already doing this through communion. When I was partaking of His blood in communion, I was receiving a powerful and active work of His blood through the practice of embracing Him. "After the same manner also he took the cup, when he had supped, saying, This cup is the new testament in my blood: this do ye, as oft as ye drink it, *in remembrance* of me" (1 Corinthians 11:25 KJV, emphasis added).

The word *remembrance* does not merely mean to reflect upon the past; it can also mean to make fresh. I was to make fresh, not have a mere memory of the past. I was to make fresh the living reality of what He has done for me today because of what He did for me in the past. I was to make fresh the active power of His blood in my life.

"For as often as you eat this bread and drink this cup, you proclaim the Lord's death till He comes" (1 Corinthians 11:26 NKJV).

The word *remembrance* means to bring forth a powerful event of the past into the present, that we may receive and apply its power in the here and now.

Baker's Evangelical Dictionary of Biblical Theology, in referring to remembrance, says it's that "which points to making present the past, so that it can be effective in the present."

This is activating a past event for an active work in the here and now—the present.

Seven key desires of His heart were presented to me as the most valuable desires that He wanted to impart into my heart. But this was not the end. It was only the beginning. There were other things in His Word that He desired for me to have and He instructed me to find them in His Word and then pray for them.

PRAYER TWO: RECEPTIVE PRAYER OF GOD'S DESIRES

Father in heaven, I receive now the infilling of your Spirit of love.

I receive now the infilling of your Spirit of righteousness.

I receive now the infilling of your Spirit of wisdom and revelation.

I receive now the infilling of your Spirit of peace.

I receive now the infilling of your Spirit of joy.

I receive you, Holy Spirit. Fill me with your presence.

I receive your blood Lord Jesus. Fill me with your blood. In your name, Lord Jesus, amen.

After the Lord revealed the seven desires of His heart for me, He then taught me to pray in an extraordinary way. He no longer wanted me to ask for these desires. Instead, He wanted me to receive them. He wanted me to use the ability and the authority He had given me for the present. He wanted me to *receive* them. He wanted me to partake of an immediate action, not a futuristic action, as implied in the word *ask*. He wanted me to use the word *receive*.

In this manner, I made myself accessible to an immediate outpouring of His magnificent presence. I was no longer expecting a divine encounter down the road, somewhere in the future. I was now positioning myself for a miraculous transformation that was to begin immediately, at the very moment I prayed this prayer.

I opened the door for an immediate response to receiving Him in the fullness of all that He is.

These are seven primary characteristics of God. What God wants us to do is pray for the release of His very character and nature into our own lives. He wants us to release the very essence of His being within our lives. He wants us to open wide the door to our hearts and receive of Him all that He has to offer.

He wants our hearts, spirits, and souls to be transformed and established with the most powerful attributes of His very own nature. If our hearts, spirits, and souls are empowered with the presence of the living God in every aspect of His self-same character, nothing will move us. No fear, no desperation, no panic, no despair, no guilt, and no condemnation will ever overwhelm us.

When our hearts, spirits, and souls are established and rooted in complete peace, surety, trust, and confidence, we cannot be moved.

When we apply this prayer of transformation, we will develop a deeper appreciation and love for the Lord Jesus Christ. As He reveals Himself more and more, we will discover a transformation process taking place within us. To be changed into His likeness requires an effort on our part to allow Him to make those changes.

Some changes are automatic when we receive Jesus as Savior into our hearts, but the deeper transformations require a more diligent effort as we seek Him for these greater and more profound changes.

God begins an immediate transformation in our lives when we become born-again children. As born-again babies, we are protected and provided for, but there comes a time when the baby must grow up. It is *how* a baby grows up that makes all the difference in the world as to what manner of success is developed. The manner in which he grows up determines whether or not he becomes a true family member or just a legal heir.

True family members operate in the power and authority of the parents through a deep-seated love relationship with the parents. Legal heirs operate in the authority and power of inheritance, through their own selfish desires, selfish ambitions, and self-promotion.

As children of God, we will make a number of choices pertaining to our relationship with our heavenly Father. We will either seek to be filled with the very presence of the Father, or we will merely seek to obtain and fill our lives with the supernatural anointings, gifts, and powers that the Father provides (that is, all the stuff that the Father owns). What should be the primary goal for wanting a relationship with Lord—to embrace the very presence of our heavenly Father or to concentrate on obtaining as many supernatural gifts and powers from Him that we possibly can? We either fill ourselves with the love of the Father and the powers of His character, *or* we aim to develop our own self-reliant characters and fill ourselves with self-willed and prideful aspirations by which we choose to live.

We choose either to exalt the presence of the Lord Jesus Christ within us, or we choose to esteem ourselves, our desires, and our determined future as more important. There can only be one person on the throne of our hearts.

Do we want to be filled with the presence of God? Or do we merely seek to be endowed with the power of God in order to fill our own lives with self-gratification and personal ambitions? This is one of the ultimate questions we must ask ourselves.

To comprehend what is gained by being filled with the presence of God is beyond our scope. To appropriate that superior state of being and to be allowed access to privileges and abilities that can only come through the appropriation of God's heavenly nature is far beyond anything that we could possibly imagine. To be filled with the fullness of God is awesome.

We have no idea of the capabilities to which we will have privilege when we are filled completely with the presence of God. Seeking to be filled with the presence of God will bring about a transformation that will allow us to become mightily empowered with supernatural abilities. Seeking the fullness of God is His greatest request of us. "Be filled" is an insightful directive of extreme importance. If we wish to live lives in the miraculous, we have no other option.

Nothing in the entire universe could ever come close to making an impression upon our lives as does being filled with the presence of God. The power of having a deep-seated love relationship with God is beyond awesome.

Without the empowerment of God's very character and nature within us, we will never be able to appropriately use the powers of heaven. If we do not have the God-given power of restraint, compassion, discernment, and love completely saturating and empowering our beings, then we will never be able to rightly handle any of the magnificent supernatural powers of heaven.

Jesus wants us to live in a love relationship with Him that is capable of releasing these powers of heaven into our lives to the fullest degree.

He wants us to become like Him in character.

He wants to fill our hearts exceedingly beyond the measure we received of Him at the time of our salvation.

We do not earn salvation; we receive it. We do not create God's love in our hearts; we receive it. We cannot, of ourselves, create the presence of God in our lives. We can only receive His transforming presence in our lives.

It is up to us to learn how to receive the manifestation of His very nature within us. He said if we draw near to Him, He will draw near to us. This is *our responsibility*.

"Draw near to God and He will draw near to you" (James 4:8 KJV, emphasis mine).

How do we draw near to God? One primary way is to learn how to receive His very character, His very presence, and His nature through prayer.

Through prayer, we can change our lives. That is why we need to learn how to pray prayers that are most effective.

Transformation is for the purpose of creating a state of being that will allow God to empower us with His presence to the fullest extent. We need to learn how to allow Him to reveal Himself in us and through us.

Prayer can bring about the establishment of a deeper relationship with the Lord. Prayer will produce a secure and unmovable spirit. Prayer will create a joining of hearts that will definitely allow us to walk on top of the most horrific and troubled seas. We need the development of God's very character within our minds, bodies, spirits, and souls.

The easiest way to overcome sin, temptation, persecution, or any disastrous circumstance that may try to overwhelm us is to seek for and allow God to establish a greater presence of Himself within us. He cannot do it, however, without our permission and perseverance to draw closer to Him.

Praying receptive prayers for the establishment of His character within us is not a one-time event. We must pray this prayer often; we should try to do so each day. This prayer will allow God to reveal Himself in and through our lives in a much greater way. As the characteristics of God's nature develop within us, an amazing demonstration of power will present itself in an ever-increasing display of strength. We indeed will discover a prayer life of power.

To receive God's love, righteousness, wisdom, revelation, peace, joy, Holy Spirit, and the powerful blood of Jesus through prayer is a most noble endeavor that will transform our lives in a most astonishing way.

Please take note: the Lord revealed there were additional virtues and characteristics that He desired of me in His Word. It was my responsibility *to read His Word and find them.* These seven were only the primary desires of His heart for me. This is what He wanted me to pray into my life.

It is up to us to search the Word of God for the rest of His desires for us. Jesus will reveal His Word and His desires for us as we search the scriptures. He will show us what to pray and how to pray for ourselves as He reveals His Word to us.

He also revealed that if I would pray His "wants" list into my life, that I would receive many of the things on my own wants list. And that is a tremendous blessing.

CHAPTER 6

THE TRANSFORMED HEART OF A SOLDIER OF LIGHT

One evening, while in prayer, I was shown in a vision a remarkably sharp-looking Roman soldier. He was well dressed in full battle array. As I gazed upon his striking appearance, I was amazed and in awe of his powerful, majestic presence, which radiated brilliant white light. From within his heart, radiating beams of light with immense power seemed to energize each piece of weaponry with a phenomenal strength. Each piece of armor seemed alive with a supernatural vitality all of its own, as if it was supercharged.

I also saw the secrets of a successful, battle-ready child of God, prepared for spiritual warfare.

HE WAS BATTLE-READY

The first thing that I noticed was that the supernatural integrity of this soldier was of the highest caliber and had everything to do with how powerful each piece of weaponry would become. This integrity originated entirely from a personal love relationship with God.

When the presence of God increased within him, each piece of armor he wore was energized and made all that much more powerful. The fullness of God radiated from within his being and into and through each piece of weaponry. He was courageous. He was fearless. He was empowered with supernatural strength. He was absolutely confident and unwavering. He was steadfast and secure. He was full of wisdom and knowledge. He was loyal and obedient to God. He was battle-ready in every area of his being.

He was empowered with the very holy nature and character of God Himself.

HE KNEW HOW TO PROTECT HIMSELF

I realized that he had a very deep and intimate love relationship with God. It was this supernatural, love-empowered relationship that provided incredible strength for this soldier. His armor had become magnificent weaponry, and these energized weapons were applied skillfully as a most impenetrable defense system for his heart. His priority was to protect his intimate relationship with God. He protected the presence of God's love that dwelled within his heart.

He was the one who held in his own hands the responsibility to protect and maintain his fellowship and relationship with God. His first duty was not to engage in battles but to defend himself, to protect himself, and to maintain himself and his relationship with God.

I saw the brilliant glow from the presence of God radiating from within this soldier's very being. I could feel the power of God's love, His peace, His joy, and His gentleness. It was overwhelming. It was wonderful. I knew that this soldier knew God—and I wanted to be just like him.

This soldier had trained his mind and his heart to develop a deep love and admiration for God. This soldier personally knew God, with supernatural intimacy of a tremendous magnitude. This soldier knew how to use his weapons of warfare as a defense.

I became aware that he used his armor for the strengthening and development of his relationship with God. This was a marvelous mystery.

He Was Prepared to Wage War

This soldier and God were of one heart, one mind, and one power. He had the mind of Christ, and he loved God with all of his heart. He had a well-grounded and established relationship with God. He was of full assurance. He had such an unmovable confidence and trust in God that whatever he set his hand to do, that is what would be accomplished and performed.

This soldier knew God. He had supernatural wisdom and knowledge. He knew how to effectively use every piece of armor in any kind of battle in which he would engage. He knew how to release the radiating power of God's presence. The light of God's power exploded with supernatural strength when a part of the armor was forced into action. The energizing effects were amazing.

I noticed he did not have any trouble with any part of the flesh. He had no problems with sin or lust. His flesh was completely subdued by the power of God's presence. His mind and his thoughts were pure. He had no trouble casting down any imagination that was contrary to God's way of thinking.

The attributes of his life were nothing short of amazing. He had a pure heart. He was able to call on the Lord and fellowship with Him easily. His priorities were established. The presence of God's love was his first priority.

"Whereas the object and purpose of our instruction and charge is love, which springs from a pure heart and a good (clear) conscience and sincere (unfeigned) faith" (1 Timothy 1:5 AMP).

He had a heart that was fearless, confident, and overflowing with a powerful assurance.

"Let us draw near with *a true heart in full assurance of faith*, having our hearts sprinkled from an evil conscience, and our bodies washed with pure water" (Hebrews 10:22 KJV, emphasis added).

He was diligent in protecting the love relationship he had with God, and he kept himself spiritually fit.

"Keep and guard your heart with all vigilance and above all that you guard, for out of it flow the springs of life" (Proverbs 4:23 AMP).

He had a spot- and blemish-free heart, a heart that was pure and clean of any sin nature. His flesh was completely subdued, free from any hint of wrongful desires or lust, and his mind was able to overcome and subdue any thought that was out of place with the righteous mind-set of Christ.

Such a person is well equipped to enter into spiritual battle and overcome anything that the devil throws at him. This person would be able to accomplish anything through prayer. The miraculous would indeed be a normal way of life.

WHAT IS THE PURPOSE OF THE ARMOR OF GOD?

"(For the weapons of our warfare are not carnal, but mighty through God to the pulling down of strong holds;) Casting down imaginations, and every high thing that exalteth itself against the knowledge of God, and bringing into captivity every thought to the obedience of Christ; And having in a readiness to revenge all disobedience, when your obedience is fulfilled" (2 Corinthians 10:4–6 KJV).

This soldier was skilled in the ability to pull down strongholds, first in his own life and then in other situations. This soldier was capable of casting down any wrong imagination with ease. He had an incredible ability to control his own thoughts. This soldier had an ability to effectively go after evil and bring it to an end. This soldier was powerful in his ability to wage supernatural warfare, and he was most successful and accomplished in all of his deeds and actions.

"Let us put on the armour of light" (Romans 13:12b KJV).

We are to grow in union in our relationship with the Lord. We are to learn how to use the armor that God provides for us that we may overcome deception and stand victorious against every one of Satan's battle plans. We must realize that we are in a battle against evil supernatural beings.

We must learn how to use the armor to defend ourselves and to resist and defeat our supernatural enemies.

> A final word: Be strong in the Lord and in his mighty power. Put on all of God's armor so that you will be able to stand firm against all strategies of the devil. For we are not fighting against flesh-and-blood enemies, but against evil rulers and authorities of the unseen world, against mighty powers in this dark world, and against evil spirits in the heavenly places. Therefore, put on every piece of God's armor so you will be able to resist the enemy in the time of evil. Then after the battle

you will still be standing firm. (Ephesians 6:10–13 NLT)

In conclusion, be strong in the Lord [be empowered through your union with Him]; draw your strength from Him [that strength which His boundless might provides]. Put on God's whole armor [the armor of a heavy-armed soldier which God supplies], that you may be able successfully to stand up against [all] the strategies and the deceits of the devil.

For we are not wrestling with flesh and blood [contending only with physical opponents], but against the despotisms, against the powers, against [the master spirits who are] the world rulers of this present darkness, against the spirit forces of wickedness in the heavenly (supernatural) sphere.

Therefore put on God's complete armor, that you may be able to resist and stand your ground on the evil day [of danger], and, having done all [the crisis demands], to stand [firmly in your place]. (Ephesians 6:10–13 AMP)

WHAT IS THE ARMOR?

Therefore put on God's complete armor, that you may be able to resist and stand your ground on the evil day [of danger], and, having done all [the crisis demands], to stand [firmly in your place]. Stand therefore [hold your ground], having tightened the belt of truth around your loins and having put on the breastplate of integrity and of moral rectitude and right standing with God, And having shod your feet in preparation [to face the enemy with the firm-footed stability, the promptness, and the readiness produced by the good news] of the Gospel of peace. Lift up over all the [covering] shield of saving faith, upon which you can quench all the flaming missiles of the wicked [one]. And take the helmet of salvation and the sword that the Spirit wields, which is the Word of God. Pray at all times (on every occasion, in every season) in the Spirit, with all [manner of] prayer and entreaty. To that end keep alert and watch with strong purpose and perseverance, interceding in behalf of all the saints (God's consecrated people). (Ephesians 6:13–18 AMP)

GIRDLE OF TRUTH

"By [speaking] the word of truth, in the power of God, with the weapons of righteousness for the right hand [to attack] and for the left hand [to defend]" (2 Corinthians 6:7 AMP).

This is not the ability to speak forth the Word of God from mere knowledge; this is the ability to release the power of God's presence into the words (His words) that you speak forth unto yourself or unto another. These are empowered words that come from a heart filled with the power and presence of God.

The most powerful words that can be uttered are spoken with the power of God's love radiating from within us. "But speaking the truth in love, may grow up into him in all things, which is the head, even Christ" (Ephesians 4:15 KJV).

"Did not our heart burn within us, while he talked with us by the way" (Luke 24:32 KJV).

God's Word comes alive within the heart, especially when it is empowered with the presence of God. Supernaturally empowered truth will touch anybody's heart.

BREASTPLATE OF RIGHTEOUSNESS

"For *with the heart man believeth unto righteousness*; and with the mouth confession is made unto salvation" (Romans 10:10 KJV, emphasis added).

"May you always be filled with the fruit of your salvation—the righteous character produced in your life by Jesus Christ—for this will bring much glory and praise to God" (Philippians 1:11 NLT).

That's what we are after—the manifestation of God's presence (His glory) within our hearts.

When we, as Christians, are born again, we receive salvation. We receive Christ's righteousness, but are we automatically filled with the fullness of His righteousness? If that were true, the apostle Paul would not have told the Christians at Philippi to continue seeking that state of being *of being filled* with the fruits of righteousness.

There are various levels of righteousness. This righteousness must be obtained, maintained, and continually sought after. We must seek that full and complete righteousness.

"This Good News tells us how God makes us right in his sight. This is accomplished from start to finish by faith. As the Scriptures say, 'It is through faith that a righteous person has life'" (Romans 1:17 NLT).

"Not having a righteousness of my own that comes from the law, but that which is through faith in Christ—the righteousness that comes from God and is by faith" (Philippians 3:9 NIV).

Having the indwelling presence of God's righteousness allows us to develop that intimate relationship with God Himself and allows us to experience the very presence and power of God. We can experience His resurrection power. We can experience the power of His supernatural life to the fullest extent.

"Blessed are they which do hunger and thirst after righteousness: for they shall be filled" (Matthew 5:6 KJV).

Love believes all things. His love believes all things. A heart filled with God's love has the ability to believe for that righteous state of being that completely satisfies.

"But seek (aim at and strive after) first of all His kingdom and His righteousness (His way of doing and being right), and then all these things taken together will be given you besides" (Matthew 6:33 AMP).

Only those who seek to be "filled" with His righteousness can become completely satisfied. Only those who are "filled" with God's righteousness will have the desires of the satisfied heart.

THE GOSPEL OF PEACE

"And let the peace (soul harmony which comes) from Christ rule (act as umpire continually) in your hearts [deciding and settling with finality all questions that arise in your minds, in that peaceful state] to which as [members of Christ's] one body you were also called [to live]. And be thankful (appreciative), [giving praise to God always]" (Colossians 3:15 AMP).

The presence of God's peace is a powerful weapon of discernment. It can determine a right from a wrong, a truth from an error, or a "go" from a "don't go" and a "do" from a "don't do" situation. The presence of God's peace is a powerful tool of discernment and guidance.

"Then you will experience God's peace, which exceeds anything we can understand. His peace will guard your hearts and minds as you live in Christ Jesus" (Philippians 4:7 NLT).

This is the most important purpose and function of the weapon of peace—to have the presence of God's supernatural power to such a degree that we will be completely secure and confident in our own salvation. This weapon of peace is more than able to eliminate and remove every speck of doubt that the devil could use against us.

This form of God's supernatural presence, His peace, will not allow us to doubt, to stumble, to backslide, or to waver in any degree of our confidence in salvation or to question the forgiveness of our sins. We will not only have the radiating power of complete and total confidence empowering our entire beings, but we also will have absolute confidence in our salvation. We will have secured a confident inner peace that is far more powerful than a mere mental conviction.

We will have complete and total confidence in our ability to do warfare against the enemy with absolute surety of obtaining complete victory and success. The natural characteristics of God's nature will empower anyone who has a steadfast confidence that is most exemplary of a fearless warrior. This confidence is so sound that we will know, with a profound assurance, that we will succeed in victory in any battle waged against us.

I saw a soldier completely empowered, with a confident peace in his heart. He knew that Lucifer would never deprive him of any victory.

"Now may the Lord of peace Himself grant you His peace (the peace of His kingdom) at all times and in all ways [under all circumstances and conditions, whatever comes]. The Lord [be] with you all" (2 Thessalonians 3:16 AMP).

"May God give you more and more grace and peace as you grow in your knowledge of God and Jesus our Lord" (2 Peter 1:2 NLT).

"May grace (God's favor) and peace (which is perfect well-being, all necessary good, all spiritual prosperity, and freedom from fears and agitating passions and moral conflicts) be multiplied to you in [the full, personal, precise, and correct] knowledge of God and of Jesus our Lord" (2 Peter 1:2 AMP).

God's peace provides perfect well-being in every area of the physical, emotional, spiritual, and material realms of our lives. God's peace will empower any soldier, any Christian, with the ability to maintain a confident journey down any path he takes, no matter what obstacles, enticements, or hardships he may encounter. God's peace is powerful in aiding the soldier to maintain his course of action without fear of straying from his objective.

SHIELD OF FAITH

"Let us draw near with a true heart in full assurance of faith, having our hearts sprinkled from an evil conscience, and our bodies washed with pure water" (Hebrews 10:22 KJV).

"For [if we are] in Christ Jesus, neither circumcision nor uncircumcision counts for anything, *but only faith activated and energized and expressed and working through love*" (Galatians 5:6 AMP, emphasis added).

Our love relationship with God has everything to do with the strength of our faith and our abilities to operate in faith. Without the presence and power of God's love flowing in and through our lives in a personal relationship with Him, our faith cannot be empowered to accomplish the greater tasks that it has been called upon to complete.

Everything in God's kingdom is a product of love. Everything in God's kingdom is a creation of love. All power in heaven and earth are a demonstration of His great and powerful love.

God's righteousness is a work of love. God's holiness is a work of love. God's justice is a work of love. It is through the power of God's love that we are set free from sin and all unrighteousness. It is through the power of His love that we are able to overcome and conquer every work of ungodliness in our lives.

God will only honor those works done in His name if they are done in the power of His love. Every work of faith must be accomplished in the power of His love. Without the presence of God's love at work in our lives, we may not receive any honor or recognition for the work we do because of the very nature in which it was produced.

Only faith that is activated and energized by the power of God's love produces reward and honor. Beware: there is a productive faith that earns no reward or honor.

"And if I have prophetic powers (the gift of interpreting the divine will and purpose), and understand all the secret truths and mysteries and possess all knowledge, and if I have [sufficient] faith so that I can remove mountains, but have not love (God's love in me) I am nothing (a useless nobody). Even if I dole out all that I have [to the poor in providing] food, and if I surrender my body to be burned or in order that I may glory, but have not love (God's love in me), I gain nothing" (1 Corinthians 13:2–3 AMP).

Can a person living in sin operate in faith? Yes, he can. Judas did. And so are the many who will cry aloud unto the Lord, "Lord, Lord, have we not prophesied in thy name? and in thy name have cast out devils? and in thy name done many wonderful works? And then will I profess unto them, I never knew you: depart from me, *ye that work iniquity*" (Matthew 7:22–23 KJV, emphasis added).

Those who deliberately choose to live in sin and who deliberately break God's laws will not be permitted into the kingdom of heaven. To know the desires of God's heart and then to deliberately choose to live in sin is rebellion. It is the same as practicing witchcraft.

The ability to operate in powerful demonstrations of faith will not guarantee salvation. Only those who love the Lord and yearn for the opportunity to please the Lord will be allowed into heaven.

A powerful ability, impressive demonstrations, anything demonstrated by faith—these are not necessarily indications of the true nature of our hearts. An impure heart that harbors sin can operate in powerful displays of faith and can fool anybody, except those who have learned how to judge, determine, and discern the presence of God's supernatural fruit within an individual's heart.

A born-again Christian can fall into and embrace (refuse to repent of) sins that will keep him or her from entering heaven, regardless of his or her ability to display supernatural feats of faith.

> For be sure of this: that no person practicing sexual vice or impurity in thought or in life, or one who is covetous [who has lustful desire for the property of others and is greedy for gain]—for he [in effect] is an idolater—has any inheritance in the kingdom of Christ and of God. Let no one delude and deceive you with empty excuses and groundless arguments [for these sins], for through these things the wrath of God comes upon the sons of rebellion and disobedience. So do not associate or be sharers with them. (Ephesians 5:5–7 AMP)

> You can be sure that no immoral, impure, or greedy person will inherit the Kingdom of Christ and of God. For a greedy person is an idolater, worshiping the things of this world. Don't be fooled by those who try to excuse these sins, for the anger of God will fall on all who disobey him. Don't participate in the things these people do. For once you were full of darkness, but now you have light from the Lord. So live as people of light! For this light within you produces only what is good and right and true. (Ephesians 5:5–9 NLT)

For this reason, it is absolutely essential to seek the Lord for a transformed heart. He can transform it. He can fortify it. He can purify it. He can heal what is broken. He can restore what was lost.

Learning how to pray for ourselves is a high priority—it should be on the top of our prayer lists.

A pure heart filled with God's love is our goal for appropriating a glorious crown of acceptance and honor as a soldier of Christ.

HELMET OF SALVATION

The helmet of salvation is a specific piece of armor that is designed to protect the head and the mind—this is important to understand. Our enemy knows well how to use psychological warfare. He is a master of brainwashing techniques. He is brilliant in the use of the power of suggestion. He is a master of deception and deceit.

Our enemy is very intelligent—far more intelligent than we give him credit. Underestimating Satan is a tragic mistake because it leaves us vulnerable.

Lucifer is highly skilled in mental manipulation—the art of persuasion and how to effectively influence an individual. Oh, he is quite ruthless when it comes to attacking our beliefs and our faith. He loves to create doubt, guilt, despair, and hopelessness. He is a master of rebellion. His most coveted prize is the separation of man from his creator, God.

One of his most infamous titles of lesser recognition is "Lord of the Flies."

CHAPTER 7

LORD OF THE FLIES

Second Kings 1:2, 3, 6—Beelzebub means "Lord of the Flies."

I will never forget one of my first teachings from the Lord on dealing with demons. It happened on a beautiful Sunday morning. A friend and I had positioned ourselves on the very front pew during the service. We were intent on listening to a rather good sermon.

Then, something most odd took place. I suddenly became aware of something flying around my head. My first thought was that it was an insect, possibly a large horsefly or something similar. It buzzed around my head again and again and then again, and I got a good look at it.

What in the world is this? I thought. It was a big, black, fuzzy thing. It had no wings or legs. It actually did not resemble an insect at all. It was just a big, black, fuzzy-looking thing about the size of a dime. It flew around my head once again, and then something most phenomenal took place. I was suddenly able to see it off to the side of my head, just as it came from behind my head. My sight was far beyond the scope of my peripheral vision—and that is when I suddenly realized that I was observing this thing with my spiritual eyes—with my spirit—as it flew around and around my head.

I did not get all bent out of shape or hysterical, but I felt quite an unexpected excitement. This thing flew around my head and stopped in midair, just off to the side of my right temple, and then, all of a sudden, it quickly entered my head.

The next thing that happened was rather mysterious. I suddenly observed a small theatrical stage directly in the front of my mind, with curtains on both sides. I saw something like a large index card being shoved on stage. It was positioned directly in front of my mind, and I read what had been clearly written.

Immediately, I blushed with embarrassment because what I had just read on that card was a disgusting, filthy thought.

As I continued observing the stage, I saw a tiny hand reach out from behind the curtain on the right side of the stage. It was trying to snatch the index card without being noticed. In its second attempt, it quickly grabbed the card and pulled it off the stage.

I was a little bit shocked but mostly amazed at what I had just experienced. In my spirit, I suddenly understood and comprehended everything that had just taken place. What I had experienced was an encounter with a little demon known as a "fly."

I realized that this thought that was placed in my mind was the result of a demonic attack on my thought life. I did not think this thought on my own. It was placed there by a little demon trained in the art of psychological warfare.

If the Holy Spirit had not plainly revealed this whole incident, I would have thought that I was the original culprit in the nasty-thought department.

The Lord taught me a most valuable lesson in supernatural deception. Demons are real. They come in all sizes.

Shortly after receiving this unique encounter, I turned toward my friend and, surprisingly, I saw a demonic fly again. This time, it flew around my friend's head. What I had just experienced was now happening to him. It flew around his head and then quickly entered his head through his temple area. He suddenly shook his head and took off his glasses. Again he shook his head, and I recognized a look of despair on his face.

I kind of chuckled because I knew what was happening. I leaned over and whispered into his ear, "You just had a dirty thought, didn't you?" He was a little alarmed and quite dumbfounded. The look on his face was that of a child caught with his hand in the cookie jar.

Quickly, he replied, "How did you know?" I could sense the unsettled concern in his voice.

Calmly, I eased his concerns and told him I would explain everything after church. Later, I taught him everything I had learned about demons known as flies. The following is what I was shown:

At sometime in your life, you probably were engrossed in reading a book, or were fully concentrating on your driving while traveling down the road, or were fully absorbed in something else you were doing. All of a sudden, out of nowhere, a thought entered your mind—you were fully absorbed in a particular train of thought and then, suddenly, a bizarre thought interrupted your concentrated focus—and it might have been a nasty thought.

Where did that thought come from?

You were not thinking about anything remotely associated with that thought, yet that thought suddenly presented itself seemingly out of thin air.

Perhaps you presented yourself before the Lord, and you entered into a session of prayer. Then, all of a sudden, thoughts of things you need to do, or family and friends, or social events suddenly enter your mind. These distractions quickly interfere with your efforts to pray. You may have encountered distracting thoughts when you were determined to spend time reading the Bible.

Where do these unexpected thoughts come from? There are tiny little demons known as flies. Their sole objective is mental manipulation through the use of persuasive thoughts. This is psychological warfare on an enormous scale. These thoughts did not originate from you. You were not concentrating on anything remotely associated with these thoughts. But they were effective in diverting you from your intended course of action.

THE GUILT TRIP

The guilt trip is a most effective tactic used to destroy a Christian's relationship with the Lord. Here is how it works: the first thought enters your mind—a nasty, ungodly thought. You are led to believe that this thought was of your own doing. You are made to feel guilty for committing sin. You are compelled to believe that you have fallen from God's grace.

Thoughts begin to flood your mind—*Now you've done it. You've committed a sin. The scripture says, as a man thinketh in his heart so is he. You've already fallen from God's grace; you might as well go ahead and sin.*

THE ASSOCIATION GAME

Another interesting trick is the association game. First, a harmless, distracting thought enters your mind. Then it leads to another harmless, distracting thought. A number of harmless thoughts may suddenly take place before the eventual nasty thought raises its ugly head. And when it does, the condemnation, guilt, and feelings of hopelessness and failure begin to overwhelm you.

In the association game, innocent thoughts eventually may lead to thoughts of those individuals who have wronged you. Before you know it, you are angry, bitter, and resentful.

Without realizing it, you have spent so much time nurturing ungodly thoughts that ungodly feelings and desires develop. Your anger has developed before you are even aware of what has happened. You have worked yourself into an ungodly frenzy, and now you feel spiritually unclean.

You have no clue as to what just took place or how to deal with the situation that has overwhelmed you.

THERE IS AN ANSWER.

There is an answer to dealing with unwanted thoughts, and it is simple. We run to the Lord. Whether guilty or not guilty of committing a sin, we run to the Lord and get it covered by the blood of Jesus.

One of the first things we must do is arm ourselves with the knowledge that these thoughts are not our thoughts. We did not conjure them up; they came out of nowhere.

When we allow these thoughts to go in one ear out the other, we did not commit any sin. The only time these thoughts become a sin is if we stop to dwell upon them, nurture them, or meditate on them.

What do we do? It is simple. The weapon of warfare that every Christian needs to put into action is the helmet of salvation. The blood of Jesus has the power to forgive. The blood of Jesus has the power to clean any soiled garment of righteousness. Every spot, every wrinkle that we acquire can be removed from our garment of righteousness.

All we have to do is run to the Lord and receive His blood, covering our sins—we simply approach Jesus and ask Him to forgive us. We can ask Him to forgive any sin, even any supposed sin that the enemy falsely accuses us of committing. And that's it. It is that simple. The power of the blood of Jesus is awesome. It keeps us clean and preserves our position of righteousness with Him. His blood restores our relationship with Him. His blood has the power to help us take control of our thought lives.

TURN SATAN'S TACTICS AGAINST HIM

Lucifer uses invasive thoughts—a powerful tool—to stir up hidden emotions and feelings of unforgiveness, hatred, and bitterness. For us to nurture these poisonous emotions is very harmful and destructive to our well-being.

This exposure could turn into a blessing, however, if it is recognized for what it is, and then we deal with it. If Satan exposes unresolved issues of forgiveness, then we can take advantage of this and get it resolved with the Lord. We can confess it and get it covered by the blood of Jesus. No matter how many times this happens, run to the Lord.

Dreams

Another way in which we can be assaulted by demonic flies is in our dreams. It takes effort to deal with these demonic dreams, but they can be overcome—and they can be stopped.

Many people have had a dream that was so filthy or ungodly that they woke up feeling dirty and unclean. Some dreams are fearful, and some are quite terrifying. There are even role-playing dreams in which we become active participants, and the wild and distasteful ending leaves us bewildered and perplexed. These dreams are skillfully created as a way to tear down our resistance and alter our behavior. They are kind of a brainwashing technique to convince us that we are exactly what we saw in our dreams. The dreams try to convince us that we are hopelessly lost sinners, unworthy of fellowship with the Lord, or that it is useless to seek the Lord for any kind of help.

These demons want us to feel as if we are doomed, with no possible way of ever going to heaven or receiving redemption. They can create a life of torment, despair, and agonizing hopelessness and misery.

There is hope, however, and there is a way of escape through the appropriation of the blood of Jesus. When we pray, "I receive your blood, Lord Jesus, over my mind," miraculous things will begin to happen.

There is power in the blood of Jesus. His blood strikes fear in the heart of *every* demonic entity. Demons cannot reside in the presence of the blood of Jesus. We must learn how to receive His blood and become filled with His blood.

In the book of Revelation 12:11, we're told, "They have defeated him by the blood of the Lamb and their testimony" (NIV).

These individuals became proficient in the appropriation and application of His blood, with a tremendous ability to overcome and defeat any evil or demonic power.

We can cleanse our consciences. We can destroy guilt, condemnation, mental anguish, and torment.

"How much more, then, will the blood of Christ, who through the eternal Spirit offered himself unblemished to God, *cleanse our consciences from acts that lead to death*, so that we may serve the living God!" (Hebrews 9:14 NIV, emphasis added),

"[In fact] under the Law almost everything is purified by means of blood, and without the shedding of blood there is neither release from sin and its guilt nor the remission of the due and merited punishment for sins" (Hebrews 9:22 AMP).

"The cup of blessing [of wine at the Lord's Supper] upon which we ask [God's] blessing, does it not mean [that in drinking it] we participate in and share a fellowship (a communion) in the blood of Christ (the Messiah)? The bread which we break, does it not mean [that in eating it] we participate in and share a fellowship (a communion) in the body of Christ?" (1 Corinthians 10:16 AMP).

All we have to do is pray a simple prayer of repentance, and ask Jesus to apply His blood to our sins. Or we can take communion and, in this way, receive His blood for the forgiveness and covering of our sins.

The most important thing is to recognize our need to run to the Lord and get our sins forgiven and covered with Jesus's blood. We can win the battle over our thought lives. Beelzebub, the Lord of the Flies, can be defeated.

The helmet of salvation is both a powerful defensive weapon used for our preservation and a powerful offensive weapon for warfare against the demonic realm.

"And almost all things are by the law *purged* with blood; and without shedding of blood is no remission" (Hebrews 9:2 KJV, emphasis added).

Purge means it has the ability to purify, to cleanse, or to sanctify. Simply put, it has the ability to clean house. His blood has all the power necessary to provide deliverance and protection.

"The cup of blessing [of wine at the Lord's Supper] upon which we ask [God's] blessing, *does it not mean [that in drinking it] we participate in and share a fellowship (a communion) in the blood of Christ (the Messiah)?* The bread which we break, does it not mean [that in eating it] we participate in and share a fellowship (a communion) in the body of Christ?" (1 Corinthians 10:16 AMP, emphasis added).

Every time we take communion, we apply the work of the blood of Jesus. We exercise the rights of purification. We apply the blood of Jesus for the purification of the mind (the thought life), the body, and the soul. We cleanse the conscience and the heart. We continue the established work of our new lives in Christ. Life is in the blood. Resurrection life is in the blood of Jesus. His blood is a purifying factor that cleanses us from all manner of sin and provides the protection needed to enter into the powerful presence of God. The power that resides within the blood of Jesus has the tremendous ability to overcome every demonic power or work of darkness.

"Let us go right into the presence of God with sincere hearts fully trusting him. *For our guilty consciences have been sprinkled with Christ's blood to make us clean,* and our bodies have been washed with pure water" (Hebrews 10:22 NIV, emphasis added).

Whenever the devil makes us feel guilty for anything, we have the knowledge and confidence that we can run to Jesus Christ and ask Him for His forgiveness. We can have a fresh start.

We can frustrate the demonic psychological warfare plans that Lucifer uses against us and stop him cold—but we must deal with it quickly. Do not ignore a demonic confrontation of any kind. Simply pray, "I receive your blood, Lord Jesus, over my mind and this situation at hand," or pray a simple prayer of forgiveness.

We must apply the blood of Jesus to the situation in one way or another. The sooner we do it, the better off we will be. To be victorious and take complete control over any situation, we must learn how to apply the blood of Jesus.

Many times, a simple prayer of repentance is all that is necessary, but there are times when taking communion provides a more in-depth work that strengthens us as well.

We are called into a personal relationship with the person who provided us with His blood and its power. Jesus Christ wants us to learn of Him and fellowship with Him. He wants us to love Him just as much as He loves us. He does not want us to use Him merely to maintain a clean life. His desire is that we recognize the power of His blood and the ability that His blood provides for developing a relationship with Him, out of a pure and clean heart. His blood provides access to a deeper relationship with Him.

When we fellowship with the Lord through communion, we can feel refreshed and clean. It is similar to feeling refreshed after stepping out of a shower after a hard day at work—but so much more. This refreshing, clean feeling encourages our hearts to fellowship with the Lord in a greater freedom. The development of a pure and clean heart will always reach into the deeper depths of His heart. Our love and affection for the Lord will increase, as will our desire to know the deeper depths of His heart and our desire to fellowship with Him.

"This cup is the new covenant [ratified and established] in My blood. Do this, as often as you drink [it], to call Me [affectionately] to remembrance" (1 Corinthians 11:25 AMP).

The basic purpose for partaking of communion is maintaining and refreshing the blood covenant of Jesus in our lives. The primary purpose, though, is to develop a personal relationship with Jesus. "To call Me [affectionately] to remembrance"—this is the primary purpose.

We make fresh a personal time of fellowship with Jesus, and this special time of fellowship is designed to restore, heal, and set free. It provides a work of restoration, and we acknowledge Jesus not just as a friend but as our high priest.

He is the high priest who sprinkles our consciences and purifies our hearts. When we receive Jesus as our high priest, we receive all of Him, the power of His blood and the power of His body.

When we reach out to Jesus—as the woman in the Matthew 9:20 reached out to touch the hem of His garment—that is when the greater miracles take place. We do not have a hem to touch, but we have Jesus, His blood, and His body.

Communion is a special time of fellowship with the Lord, as friend and as high priest. It is a special time of restoration and of receiving the miraculous power of His blood and His body.

Communion is a special event that will develop our ability to receive. Although the ability to receive is really simple, it is difficult for many to accomplish. This is why we need to practice taking communion, so that we may grow and develop receptive minds and spirits. That we may receive every kind of miracle and blessing that Jesus has provided us is, indeed, His miracle for us.

Jesus provided a special time—communion—so that we may receive and learn to receive Him as the restoring high priest.

The blood of Jesus has powerful deliverance abilities when we face any undesirable circumstance in our lives. It has the power to deliver from spiritual death and sin and from the very presence of evil. His blood can provide us with the power and the strength to cast down and cast out every ungodly influence or stronghold that attacks us, mentally or spiritually. The blood of Jesus has tremendous power to deliver any heart from resentment, bitterness, hatred, and evil of any kind.

The blood of Jesus saves, purifies, restores, protects, delivers, forgives and forgets. The power of the blood of Jesus is a mighty weapon used for creating, establishing, and maintaining our spiritual lives. The blood of Jesus is the power source that enables us to have our pasts wiped clean and to create a new beginning— no matter how many times we may falter, slip, or fall.

The blood of Jesus is like a fountain of youth. His blood is life-refreshing, life-energizing, and life-renewing. His blood helps us to maintain clean and pure hearts, completely spotless and blemish-free.

With a clean heart, God can reveal His presence to us in a number of magnificent ways that are beyond our comprehension. He loves to dwell within a clean heart.

Many healing testimonies have occurred during participation of communion. The body and the blood of Jesus provide health and healing as well.

SWORD OF THE SPIRIT

"For the Word that God speaks is alive and full of power [making it active, operative, energizing, and effective]; it is sharper than any two-edged sword, penetrating to the dividing line of the breath of life (soul) and [the immortal] spirit, and of joints and marrow [of the deepest parts of our nature], exposing and sifting and analyzing and judging the very thoughts and purposes of the heart. And not a creature exists that is concealed from His sight, but all things are open and exposed" (Hebrews 4:12–13 AMP).

When the Word of God is energized with God's supernatural presence, it becomes a most powerful tool and weapon. It is a powerful tool when it is used to expose our innermost thoughts and desires, as well as the innermost thoughts and desires of others. This is a wonderful thing when it opens the eyes of others to their need to receive Jesus into their lives. On the other hand, it is a powerful weapon of judgment upon those who rebel and wage war against Christ. The Word of God will arise as a testimony against everything it has exposed within the heart of an individual.

The condition of the heart plays an important role in how effective the Word of God is demonstrated in our lives. A heart with any bitterness, hate, unforgiveness, or greed will *always* greatly limit how the Word of God will perform; *we will be severely limited* in what the empowered Word of God could do in our lives. The manifestation of miracles to our prayer lives could be hindered greatly.

There are times, however, when God will intervene in our behalf, despite the condition of our hearts, especially; when a miraculous intervention is intended for another.

A heart that is anything less than pure will always be a hindrance. A heart that is not pure is not capable of handling the Word of God with perfection. Too many Christians are wielding the sword as they see fit, with corrupted hearts.

God desires to dwell within the entire heart. He does not want to share any space with any kind of sin. Your heart needs a good cleansing with the blood of Jesus and the Word of God.

"All Scripture is inspired by God and is useful to teach us what is true and to make us realize what is wrong in our lives. It corrects us when we are wrong and teaches us to do what is right. God uses it to prepare and equip his people to do every good work" (2 Timothy 3:16–17 NLT).

Before we use the scripture to correct others, we must use the Word of God to correct, teach, prepare, and equip ourselves. The *first* application of the empowered Word of God is for the reconditioning of our own hearts, which need to be taught, corrected, and disciplined. The heart needs to be instructed in the works of righteousness. We need to understand how God thinks and learn of His desires.

We are about to travel to a new world, in which the way of living is far different from ours. It is a culture that is pure, righteous, and holy. The people who live there are beings of righteousness. They have pure hearts filled with the glorious presence of God. This is a society that is wholly absorbed in the presence of God's powerful, radiating love and lives in the powerful demonstrations of the miraculous. Everyone is able to use extraordinary faith in all of their daily activities.

The process of transformation begins the very second we become born-again Christians. Learning to live in supernatural love, peace, and holiness is not something that can happen overnight. It is not something that automatically develops when we arrive in heaven. It begins here on earth when we accept Jesus Christ as Lord and Savior.

The ability to fellowship with God in His world will be incredible. We must not wait, however, until we get to heaven to begin. We can experience His love here on earth. We can begin a transformation process that will help us along in our adaptation into His world.

If we can think as God thinks (because God is king of His world), then we can begin to understand Him, come to love Him, and desire the same things that He desires. To be able to think like Him and desire the same things that He desires is absolutely necessary. It will make all the difference In the present world in which we live. Knowing when or how to pray for a miracle or supernatural intervention is important. Learning how to correctly use the power of faith for miraculous demonstrations is crucial. God does not want dangerous Christians turned loose in the world, especially in His world. Ignorant, undisciplined, and untrained Christians could be considered very dangerous and destructive.

To gain a clear understanding of God, we need to explore the scriptures pertaining to His character and His nature. We need to learn of His desires and discover His desires for us. We need to discover the love that He has for us, and we need to discover the answer to a most important question: why does He love us? Why does He think we are so important that He would send His Son to earth to die for us and save us from eternal damnation?

The answer unfolds when we discover what kind of a being He is. He is a being of love, not merely a being that has love. He is an all-powerful, supernatural being that is love. There is a supernatural force—an intelligence—that exists beyond the regions of our universe and that supersedes anything we can comprehend. There is a being that is so powerful that He can manipulate any galaxy and any solar system that we can observe. He is so powerful that with one hand, He can crush or create a galaxy. He is made up of powerful energies of love, of which we have only scratched the surface in their discoveries.

To grasp what kind of being He is, we need to take a look in the book of Genesis. The first thing we discover is a being of incredible power.

In Genesis 1:3-29, we see, "Then God said, 'Let there be light,' and there was light. Then God said, 'Let there be firmament …' Then God said, 'Let the waters under the heavens be gathered together into one place.] Then God said, 'Let there be lights in the firmament of the heavens.' Then God said, 'Let the waters abound with abundance of living creatures. Then God said, 'Let the earth bring forth the living creature according to its kind.' Then God said, 'Let Us make man in Our image.' *And God Saw"* (emphasis added).

What did God see? He saw what He said. He saw what He spoke into existence. His Word, empowered with His presence, is so powerful that whatever He says will be created and come into existence. Can you imagine a being of such intelligence and genius that He can design complex creations within His mind and heart and then speak them into existence?

How does this relate to us? God wants us to become like Him. He wants us to think and act like Him. He wants us to take on His character and His nature so that we may be able handle His Word wisely and in the power of His Spirit. He wants us to work and accomplish great things, to be creative and successful, and to be victorious in everything we do.

Consider Joshua, a man of God, who spoke to the sun and the moon, commanding them to stand still in the middle of the day. Frozen in time for about a full day our entire planetary system obeyed the command of a man. Through this magnificent feat a great victory was won. (Joshua 10:12-13).

If we could grasp the significance of such a God empowered faith, our lives would change forever. Christ said that if we had an amount of faith that was only the size of a mustard seed, we could speak to mountains and see them move. Moving mountains is just kindergarten abilities. If we had faith that was only half the size of mustard seed, could we possibly imagine what kind of powerful prayer life we would have?

"Then Jesus told them, 'I tell you the truth, if you have faith and don't doubt, you can do things like this and much more. You can even say to this mountain, "May you be lifted up and thrown into the sea," and it will happen. You can pray for anything, and if you have faith, you will receive it'" (Matthew 21:21–22 NLT).

"For assuredly, I say to you, whoever *says* to this mountain, 'Be removed and be cast into the sea,' and does not doubt in his heart, but believes that those things he says will be done, he will have whatever he says. Therefore I say to you, whatever things you ask when you pray, believe that you receive them, and you will have them" (Mark 11:23–24 NKJV, emphasis added).

Note that the word *says* in the previous verse holds with it a meaning of determination. It means to say and keep on saying until that mountain moves. There is willpower and persistence in the use of our faith. Remember, we are the ones who are in training. Remember the old saying: "Practice makes perfect."

God wants us to be like Him in the power of His might and of His faith abilities. God desires that we should be children who desire to be like their heavenly Father. He wants us to pattern our abilities, our lifestyles, our characters, and our natures after Him. These things are necessary if we are ever to be trusted with such power. This is why we need a complete overhaul—to be transformed into His likeness—and we need His help to do it. And this is something for which we can pray.

"The Lord your God will change your heart and the hearts of all your descendants, so that you will love him with all your heart and soul and so you may live!"* (Deuteronomy 30:5, NLT emphasis added)

To be like God—to be children in His likeness—is to have a heart transformed by Him and filled with His supernatural presence.

If we are to learn how to speak like Him, we must have the power of His presence and His authority residing within us. Then when we speak, the brick walls in our lives will crumble, the miraculous will become a way of life, and victory will triumph over our supernatural enemies.

CHAPTER 8

FRUIT OF THE HOLY SPIRIT

Our hearts not only need transformation, but they also need to be filled with the Holy Spirit and His fruit. The ability to acquire His gifts or His abilities are nothing in comparison to His desire for the development of His supernatural fruit within our hearts.

When we receive the Holy Spirit within our hearts, the seeds for transformation are planted, but the growth process is totally up to us. We can nurture its growth, or we can restrict its growth.

The fruit that develops from the presence of the Holy Spirit within us is "love, joy, peace, patience, kindness, goodness, faithfulness, gentleness, and self-control" (Galatians 5:22–23 NIV).

The emotions and feelings that man demonstrates within his life cannot compare to the empowered emotions and feelings of the Holy Spirit. You see, the fruit of the Holy Spirit is supernaturally empowered. This is a love, joy, and peace that is so overwhelmingly powerful that it exceeds anything we can comprehend. It is beyond comprehension; it is that powerful.

All of His fruit is supernaturally empowered, and great supernatural strength resides in His fruit. With this comes an incredible ability to show forth the character and nature of God. Once we receive Jesus as Lord and Savior, the transformation process by the Holy Spirit begins.

"Therefore *be imitators of God* [copy Him and follow His example], as well-beloved children [imitate their father]" (Ephesians 5:1 AMP, emphasis added).

We are to walk in love, just as Christ loved us (Ephesians 5:2).

Hearts filled with the power of His supernatural fruit will enable us to walk with God in the power of His Spirit. Think of the ability to walk in the *full power* and *demonstration* of the fruit of the Holy Spirit.

"Walk as children of light: (For the fruit of the Spirit is in all goodness and righteousness and truth ;) Proving what is acceptable unto the Lord" (Ephesians 5:8–10 KJV).

There is great need to have a transformed heart that is of similar character and nature to God Himself. Powerful supernatural gifts do not produce fruit; they are only demonstrations of abilities, a mere display of supernatural tools.

For example, the placement of a power drill in our hands does not create godly character within our hearts. The only thing that the power drill will do is magnify and produce a work that is of the true nature of whatever exists in our hearts.

If our hearts are filled with bitterness or anger, then the power drill will produce an evidence of that. The work quality will demonstrate the emotions of the heart.

If our hearts are filled with godly love, then the quality of work will demonstrate great care and accuracy.

This is why there is a great need for a transformation of our hearts. By praying for the desires of God's heart into our own hearts, we allow the Holy Spirit to develop and produce His fruit in our lives. This transforming process is nothing short of amazing—and we can pray for it.

The fruit of the Holy Spirit produces a pure and holy heart and the character and nature of God. The fruit of the Holy Spirit will produce the godly individual that He so desires.

As the fruit of the Holy Spirit increases within us, the desires of the flesh will decrease. An incredible way to crucify the flesh and its desires is to pursue the presence of the Holy Spirit. The more we seek to be filled with the Holy Spirit, the easier it will become to overcome every desire of the flesh—every corrupt and ungodly desire can be overcome.

As the fruit of the Holy Spirit develops within our hearts, a powerful transformation begins to take place. It is the power of His fruit that makes the person. As the power of His fruit is demonstrated in our lives, we will have no trouble being identified as true men and women of God. The Holy Spirit provides a light within us that can be seen and recognized. Though rarely seen with the naked eye, many will be drawn to us because of what they sense or spiritually see. Then again, some people—those who embrace the darkness and hate the light—will become hostile toward us because of what they sense or spiritually see.

There are prophets out there who are totally fruitless. They have been given a power gift to operate, but upon close examination, we can see that the light of the Holy Spirit is not within them. Many talented preachers are fruitless. There is no light of the Holy Spirit within them. Many Christians who sit in a church pew every Sunday are fruitless. There is no light of the Holy Spirit within them. Many claim authority and positions of prominence, but they are as dead men walking. Just because they have a power tool placed in their hands does not mean that they are godly men or women.

The disciple Judas Iscariot is a good example. He was given authority to operate in the supernatural gifts. He ate with Jesus. He slept with Jesus. He worked with Jesus. He was given authority to preach the gospel, heal the sick, and cast out demons. Judas did all of these things; he used the power tools, but his heart was not for the Lord. He had his own agenda, and he sought to perform his own work to build the kingdom of God. He had a great love for the gifts and the abilities he was given—the things of God—but his love for the Lord Himself was not on the top of his list.

If he truly had loved the Lord, he would not have taken it upon himself to try to lead the Lord into victory. Instead, he would have followed the Lord into victory. Only an intimate love relationship with Jesus would have created the desire in Judas's heart to follow Jesus.

As a born-again believer, you must ask yourself a most important question: are you a legal heir, or are you a family member?

A Christian who does not seek the Lord or the Holy Spirit for a transformed heart will merely walk in the desires of his flesh. Without gaining spiritual insight from a transformed heart, he cannot accomplish the desires of God's heart. He will not know how to follow the Lord into victory. Instead, he will try to use his supernatural tools to lead Jesus into victory, just as the disciple Judas did. This is a fatal mistake.

Sadly, all that many Christians want of a future life is a place reserved for them in heaven. They have no desire to know the Lord or even love Him. They are highly attracted to obtaining all the blessings, supernatural gifts, talents, and anointing they can get. They only develop a relationship with the things they can appropriate from God, but there is no effort made to sit in the Lord's presence and get to know Him. There is no love relationship with the Lord; He is only a business partner that provides things. A legal heir is only after the things of God.

A true family member is one who seeks a personal love relationship with the Lord. Only a heart in the process of transformation can come to know and experience a pure relationship of love with the Lord.

Please keep in mind that we can pray for God's help to recreate or transform our hearts. We can pray for that relationship of love with Him. No matter how hard or cold our hearts may have become, through prayer they can be transformed.

If hearts are not right with God, then the work they perform will not be right. Their work will demonstrate, in one way or another, the reflection of what is really in their hearts. I have seen fruitless prophets do more damage than good. I have seen talented ministries go to the wayside because they allowed the fruit that once blossomed in their hearts to go to ruin. I have seen many Christians falter and backslide because they let the presence of the Holy Spirit dry up in their hearts.

We cannot give what we do not have. If God's love is not present in our lives, then we cannot share it. We can share truth, but presenting the truth without the presence of God's love will not allow His Word to burn within our hearts.

It is simple: if we don't have the powerful presence of God's fruit in our lives, then that reality of life cannot be shared. His love is a powerful supernatural fruit.

When was the last time you read the Bible and the words seemed to jump off the page with amazing insight that filled your heart and mind with wonder?

When was the last time your heart was flooded with incredible insight and understanding pertaining to the remarkable character and nature of God?

When was the last time the eyes of your heart were enlightened with insightful revelations of God's wonderful kingdom in heaven?

When was the last time your heart was filled with the amazing warmth of His love?

It is a rare and difficult situation to experience any of these without a transformed heart or a heart that is in the process of change. To experience the presence of God's amazing love is a remarkable wonder beyond anything we could possibly imagine.

The spiritual realm is real—so very real. A true spiritual relationship with the Lord allows us the opportunity to experience Him. The powerful presence of His love is awesome, but so is the ability to touch His mind.

In an instant, He can reveal something so incredible that it would take us hours—even days—to write it all out. No computer in the world could ever come close to His ability to transfer data and information. His thought processes are very fast, and His thoughts are filled with insightful wonder.

What I think is an astonishing miracle, in and of itself, is that anyone can enjoy and experience this kind of relationship with Him. We just need to give Him a little bit of our time and seek Him for a transformed heart—that is the wonderful part.

With the Holy Spirit radiating the power of God through the fruit that has been produced in our hearts, our hearts will be warmed and convicted by His presence when we share the Word of God.

This is one of the most important reasons for pursuing the transformation of our hearts—and we can pray for it. Don't simply sit and wait for it to happen. Pursue it. Go after it. Receive it.

Let's put ourselves on the top of our prayer lists and pray for the transformation of our hearts.

CHAPTER 9

PRAYER OF RESTORATION AND RENEWAL

THE COMMUNION PRAYER: A PRAYER OF DELIVERANCE, RESTORATION, AND HEALING

The main purpose of the communion prayer is to practice a continual refreshing of the blood and the body of Jesus Christ so that deliverance, healing, and restoration may take place in our lives.

If we are wounded or broken, Jesus can fix and restore us through the power of His body and blood. Through communion, we can activate the powerful virtues of Christ's blood and body in our lives. Through His blood and body, we can receive deliverance, restoration, and healing.

"This cup is the new covenant in my blood; do this, whenever you drink it, *in remembrance* of me" (I Corinthians 11:25 NIV emphasis added).

"And when he had given thanks, he brake it, and said, Take, eat: this is my body, which is broken for you: this do *in remembrance* of me" (1 Corinthians 11:24 KJV, emphasis added).

Again, Luke confirms : "After the same manner also he took the cup, when he had supped, saying, This cup is the new testament in my blood: this do ye, as oft as ye drink it, *in remembrance* of me" (Luke 22:19 KJV, emphasis added).

I cannot emphasize enough the importance of our ability to apply the powerful blood of Jesus in our life. To activate the powerful blood of Jesus we must "make present the past, so that it can be effective in the present".

In essence it is making fresh the working power of Jesus's blood and body, provided by Him on the cross.

When we soil our garments of righteousness with sin, the only way we can clean our garment is with a fresh application of the blood of Jesus.

The word *remembrance* truly means to make fresh the power of the past for the present.

What are we making fresh in our lives when we take communion? We are actively applying a new and fresh work of the sin-cleansing and life-empowering work of the blood of Jesus. The blood of Jesus Christ provides a powerful work of *deliverance* and *restoration*. The power of the body of Christ provides a powerful work of *healing* and *wholeness*.

At the Passover in Egypt, the application of the blood provided protection from all the elements of death. The death angel could not touch or hinder the people in any way. When the Israelites ate the body of the Lamb, they were all healed. Partaking of the body of the Lamb provided health and healing of their physical bodies. There was not one feeble person among them when they left Egypt.

We actively apply and receive all the healing virtues of the body of Christ when we partake of the bread that represents His body. We receive His healing virtues for our physical, emotional, mental, and spiritual well-being. For this reason, many who do not recognize the power of deliverance in the blood of Christ or the healing virtues of the body of Christ when they partake of communion fail to receive deliverance and healing in their lives. Understand that it is not the Lord's will that we should die before our time.

"He who eats My flesh and drinks My blood abides in Me, and I in him" (John 6:56 NKJV).

"The cup of blessing which we bless, is it not the communion of the blood of Christ? The bread which we break, is it not the communion of the body of Christ?" (1 Corinthians 10:16 NKJV).

When we partake of Communion, we develop a relationship with the Lord that allows Him to reveal Himself within us in an entirely new and refreshing way. As we feast upon (fellowship, intimately embrace) Jesus and His resurrection power, we will receive the healing virtues that He has provided for us. We will develop a deeper intimacy with Jesus as our sanctifier and healer. Jesus has provided for us His blood and His body for the purpose of maintaining deliverance from evil, providing restoration, and appropriating health and healing. The sanctifying power of His blood in our lives provides an ability to keep our garments of righteousness clean, spotless, and free of any wrinkles. His blood provides supernatural life that directly affects our physical, mental, and emotional well-being. His blood provides a powerful supernatural work of deliverance from every kind of evil influence.

In His blood resides a supernatural power that separates every evil influence from our being. The power of the supernatural life that emanates from His blood provides freedom from every evil influence that tries to control our lives. Evil imaginations, tormenting dreams, vile feelings, shameful passions, and demonic attacks on our person—every sort of evil that attempts to cling to us can be cut off and separated from us forever through the powerful application of the blood of Jesus.

The blood of Jesus provides the power of life. God said, "Life is in the Blood." The life-giving power of the blood of Jesus has the power to overcome death and everything that leads to death. With the renewing of the power of the blood of Jesus in our lives, all the negative influential powers that pull at our flesh, emotions, and desires can be subdued and overcome. The works of death have to flee at the presence of the life-giving power of

Jesus's blood. That is why we need to continually make fresh the application of Jesus's blood and body in our lives.

Many people pray all manner of curses, death, and destruction upon us every day. They pray for the release of every base and despicable demonic influence. They pray for the release of demonic traps and snares to overwhelm and overpower us. This is why it is important to realize the significance of communion and that there is great benefit in refreshing ourselves with the life-giving power and deliverance-working power of Jesus's blood and body.

Communion is a continual process of discovery. Every time we partake of communion, we provide a special opportunity for the Lord Jesus Christ to minister to us. It also provides a special opportunity for us to minister to Him.

When Jesus makes a fresh and spotless garment or provides a healing, we cannot but adore Him and honor Him with thanksgiving. In this manner, Jesus is able to reveal Himself to us in yet another marvelous way. The active application of the blood of Jesus provides power for deliverance from everything ungodly and evil. The active application of the body of Jesus provides restoration and healing for our minds, bodies, spirits, and souls. If we have been wounded or injured by the effects of sin, communion can provide restoration.

When we partake of communion, we are commanded to discern the purpose for which we take it.

Therefore whoever eats this bread or drinks this cup of the Lord in an unworthy manner will be guilty of the body and blood of the Lord. But let a man examine himself, and so let him eat of the bread and drink of the cup. For he who eats and drinks in an unworthy manner eats and drinks judgment to himself, not discerning the Lord's body.

For this reason many are weak and sick among you, and many sleep. For if we would judge ourselves, we would not be judged. But when we are judged, we are chastened by the Lord, that we may not be condemned with the world.

Therefore, my brethren, when you come together to eat, wait for one another. But if anyone is hungry, let him eat at home, lest you come together for judgment. And the rest I will set in order when I come. (1 Corinthians 11:27–34 NKJV)

What do we discern?
What do we examine?
What do we judge?

It is the motive in which we partake of communion. Our motives should be for the purpose of maintaining a clean garment, for appropriating health and healing, and for applying the life-giving power of His blood to overcome the powers of evil and sin.

There is a purpose for taking communion, and if we remain ignorant of God's provisional methods to be blessed of Him, then we will fail to receive of Him.

The Lord has strongly encouraged us to practice communion. Communion provides many benefits—miraculous healings, deliverances, cleansings, and refreshing from the Lord are numerous. Many miracles happen when we practice the taking of the blood of Jesus and His body. Communion is a very desirable practice.

CHAPTER 10

HAVING A DESIRE TO SIN

If you are living in sin, and you recognize that you have wrong desires within you that pull at your intellect, emotions, feelings, and flesh, inciting you to sin, then know that God has provided a way of escape through His Son.

Communion can provide deliverance from sin and create new desires of righteousness and holiness. You may be living in sin, or sin may have a stronghold on your mind, body, or soul, but if you desire to be set free from this sin, then take communion—and continue doing so until you are set free. Anyone who is willing to let go of and release any kind of sin or sinful desire can be set free through communion.

The blood of Jesus provides deliverance from sin and help for the securing of a holy lifestyle. Communion produces a work of removing every sin and every sinful desire that may abide within you. Receiving the supernaturally empowered work of the blood of Jesus will produce a work of deliverance and cleansing from sin, *and* it will enforce judgment upon that sin—a judgment of separation!

When a judgment of separation takes place upon sin in your life, let go of that sin. It could be very costly if you continue to embrace any sin that is being separated from you by God's presence. You must not fight against or resist the power of the blood of Christ. You must be willing to let the Lord perform a work of sin separation. Do not stand up in defiance and declare, "I won't let go of this sin. I don't care what you think. I'm not giving it up." In doing so, you are declaring that you love the sin more than you love the Lord. That could be costly for you.

CHAPTER 11

GIVING YOU GODLY DESIRE AND POWER

Dear friends, you always followed my instructions when I was with you. And now that I am away, it is even more important. Work hard to show the results of your salvation, obeying God with deep reverence and fear. For God is working in you, giving you the desire and the power to do what pleases him.

> Do everything without complaining and arguing, so that no one can criticize you. Live clean, innocent lives as children of God, shining like bright lights in a world full of crooked and perverse people. Hold firmly to the word of life; then, on the day of Christ's return, I will be proud that I did not run the race in vain and that my work was not useless. (Philippians 2:12–17 NLT)

God will create new desires within our hearts—if we let Him. He will create desires for righteousness and holiness. He will provide us with supernatural power that will enable us to accomplish those things that He desires of us.

"For God is working in you, giving you the desire and the power to do what pleases him" (Philippians 2:12–13 NLT).

Having wrong desires or motives of the heart or having a heart that is unwilling to serve the Lord can be changed with His help. We cannot change our hearts; only God can change our hearts and our desires.

Realize, though, that we must seek Him for this change.

King David prayed for a new heart. "Create in me a clean heart Oh, God and renew a right spirit within me" (Psalm 51:10 KJV). He also prayed for the renewal, a cleansing of his spirit.

One of the most important lessons that I learned from the Lord is that whenever I sought to change my heart through every means and method I could think of, I always ended up a miserable failure. Whenever I turned to the Lord, however, and pursued Him for a change of heart, that was when the changes of my heart occurred. He was the one who provided the successful renovations of my heart.

There was a time in my life when my love for the Lord dwindled to practically nothing. I desperately wanted to renew and regain that deep love relationship with the Lord that I once had. Oh, how I missed that greater fullness of His love in my heart. My heart seemed to have turned to stone, and I hated it.

With diligence I tried praying more, reading the Bible more, and praising Him more. I did everything I could think of to recreate a loving heart toward the Lord.

I failed miserably. Then one day, in utter frustration, I gave up. I finally approached the Lord for His help. Everything I'd tried to do to change my heart condition ended in failure. This is when He provided a most profound revelation: "Do you realize what you were doing? You were spending so much time trying to change your heart condition that you completely overlooked the one who could change your heart for you."

What a revelation! When I started seeking after the Lord Himself for the creation of appropriate desires within my heart, my heart then began a process of change.

When we truly seek the person of Jesus Christ through communion, the miracles will come.

Jesus is not a faded memory of someone who lived in the past. He is alive—now, in the present. His life is full of glorious power and living energy. We are not partaking of a dead person. We are partaking of a person who radiates His powerful presence through blood that is alive and active in the here and now.

We are partaking of blood that is saturated with tremendous supernatural power and of a body that continually radiates the awesome power of God's glory. Awesome powers of deliverance and healing reside in the blood and the body of Jesus Christ. This is why communion is so important.

We drink His blood. We eat His body. We actively receive the person of Jesus Christ into our lives for the creation and establishment of the most awesome relationship that we could ever possibly have.

We must diligently seek Him for the changes necessary in our lives that will enable us to commune with Him on His level. He wants us to become transformed so that we will be able to enter into a supernatural way of life that is superior in every way to that which we now know life to be.

Jesus reached down to us on our level in order to bring us up to His level. Through transformation, Jesus wants us to become like Him. He wants us to become a person living in and filled with the supernatural presence and power of God Himself.

We must diligently reach out to Him from our hearts to know Him.

The blood of Jesus provides power to accomplish two amazing things:

1. The blood of Jesus provides the cleansing power to forgive the sinner. It provides mercy for the sinner. It maintains a garment of righteousness that is free from any spot or blemish.

2. The blood of Jesus provides the power of deliverance. The blood of Jesus provides a supernatural power to resist and overcome every kind of temptation, sin, or situation. Any sin or desire to sin that we wish to have separated from

our beings can be dealt with and removed. If we desire to live a clean life, His blood can provide that.

Restoration of our whole being is our goal. To do this we must be willing to accept the Lord's help in our transformation.

For those who say, "I desire to sin, but I know that these yearnings need to be removed from my life," take communion. Jesus will create greater desires for holiness.

The blood of Jesus has the power of eternal life and the ability to restore our garments of righteousness. His blood will clean and remove every spot or blemish that has soiled our garments. The blood of Jesus creates brand-new beginnings. The blood of Jesus will produce a new state of being that is required for a pure and holy relationship with Him.

All sin will be judged. Sin was judged in our lives when we first received Jesus as our Lord and Savior. We were cleansed and set free from all sin at that specific point. It is possible, however, to mess up and fall back into sin unexpectedly. Communion or a prayer of repentance will restore our blemished and spotted garments of righteousness. Communion helps to establish and restore a holy lifestyle.

The spilled blood of Abel (Adam and Eve's son) cried out for justice.

"The voice of your brother's blood cries out to Me from the ground" (Genesis 4:10 NKJV).

But the blood of Jesus speaks of better things.

"Jesus the Mediator of the new covenant, and to the blood of sprinkling that speaks better things than that of Abel" (Hebrews 12:24 NKJV).

The blood of Jesus does not speak out for revenge or justice. His blood speaks of redemption, forgiveness, and mercy. Jesus wants everybody to be cleansed and saved. But the problem is that not everybody wants Jesus to cleanse or forgive them. Many stubbornly choose to live in sin and ungodly desires. They do not want to change. They do not want their hearts to be transformed. They do not want to become like Jesus. They do not want a relationship with Him.

There must be repentance, a change of mind, and a change in the desire of the heart to live in spiritual freedom from sin. We must choose, no matter what the condition or the situation in our lives, to receive the mind of Christ (to be like-minded) and to receive and experience His desires so that we may walk in righteousness.

The blood of Jesus provides the power to cleanse us from sin, guilt, and despair. His blood provides the means in which we can approach God and experience His presence. The blood of Jesus provides holiness, speaks of mercy for the sinner, and provides the power for the separation of sin from our lives. This is what allows us to approach God.

God never forces anyone to seek a holy lifestyle. This is a lifestyle that we must choose of our own free will.

Our lifestyles are of our own choosing—and so are the consequences of what we choose. We either choose to seek a holy life, free from sin, or we choose to suffer the consequences of the sin that we hold onto and receive the judgments that it produces.

CHAPTER 12

THIS IS WHY WE TAKE COMMUNION

"Then Jesus said to them, 'Most assuredly, I say to you, unless you eat the flesh of the Son of Man and drink His blood, you have no life in you. Whoever eats My flesh and drinks My blood has eternal life, and I will raise him up at the last day. For My flesh is food indeed, and My blood is drink indeed. He who eats My flesh and drinks My blood abides in Me, and I in him'" (John 6:53–57 NKJV).

Communion is a special time of prayer that fortifies the new covenant of Jesus Christ in our lives. It is a life-changing prayer that makes fresh the miraculous power of His blood and His body.

Once we have received salvation, it is our duty to keep our wedding garments clean. If we indulge in sin, our wedding garments will be stained with spots and blemishes.

"Yet you still have a few [persons'] names in *Sardis who have not soiled their clothes*, and they shall walk with Me in white, because they are worthy and deserving" (Revelation 3:4 AMP, emphasis added).

"Therefore … purchase from Me … white clothes to clothe you and to keep the shame of your nudity from being seen, and salve to put on your eyes, that you may see. Those whom I [dearly and tenderly] love, I tell their faults and convict and convince and reprove and chasten [I discipline and instruct them]. So be enthusiastic and in earnest and burning with zeal *and repent* [changing your mind and attitude]" (Revelation 3:18–19 AMP, emphasis added).

The Apostle Paul refers to Christians who allowed their wedding garments to become dirty. They have fallen or committed acts of sin. Then, again, he speaks of Christians that have lost their garment of righteousness. More than likely these are Christians that have chosen to embrace and live in sin. They stand naked in need of appropriate clothing to cover themselves. Again, he speaks of Christians that become blind. They have lost their vision, their ability to see. The ability to spiritually see or receive revelation has been obstructed.

Only the blood and body of Christ can clothe, restore, and make whole.

It does not make any difference how big or how small a sin we commit; all sin is dirty and will produce a spot, blemish, or wrinkle in our garments. It does not matter whether our sin is deliberate or done in ignorance. Sin will always discolor our beautiful garment of white.

Jesus provided a way for us keep our garments clean. By His blood, our garments can be renewed. Our garments can once again radiate the brilliance of pure white. If our spiritual wedding garments become stained with sin, we must ask the question, "To what degree will the Lord overlook dirty wedding garments?"

"Blessed (happy and to be envied) *are those who cleanse their garments*, that they may have the authority and right to [approach] the tree of life and to enter through the gates into the city" (Revelation 22:14 AMP, emphasis added).

This permissive world has accepted many sinful pleasures as a normal way of life and insists that Christians do the same. When Christians yield to sin and stain their white garments, many will become guilt-ridden or rebellious.

Instead of pursuing the necessary actions that will cleanse their garments, they will create rational excuses to ease their consciences. They will strive to make allowances for what they did and for what they want to continue doing.

We may choose to make allowances for all of our ungodly spots and blemishes, but overlooking what we may consider insignificant does not necessarily mean that God will consider it insignificant. When we maintain a desire to sin, *we seem to make every excuse for our sins and make no attempt to seek God for His help in overcoming them.* And here lies the tragedy. Today's modern Christians want to go to heaven; they want to be saved and have a place reserved for them at the wedding feast of God, but they do not want to repent of their sins.

They are not willing to make a determined decision to do what is right. They are not willing to overcome and subdue their emotions or desires to sin. They are not willing to do what they know is the right thing to do. They are not willing to seek God's hand of intervention to overcome and remove their special strongholds or sins that they recognize and enjoy in their lives. They choose to accept the standards of the world over God's standards. They choose to base their spirituality on new guidelines that the world has reinvented. They do this mainly because they do not want to give up their sinning. They enjoy it too much.

Many born-again Christians do not want to live a life of holiness. This is due, in part, to misconceived ideas that Satan has implanted within their hearts about what living a holy lifestyle is all about. They do not know the truth.

Nevertheless, they are not willing to repent.

Most Christians are taught that repentance is an act of being remorseful and sorry for their sins. Though this is desirable, it is not enough in most cases. The word *repent* in the Bible refers to an individual who deliberately sets his mind, his will, his feelings, and his emotions on a course of action directed toward a pure and holy lifestyle that is the only way of life permitted in heaven. Our destination is heaven, and our goal is to receive a transformed life that is of the same nature and character as that of God. We are to set our vision and focus on heaven and our own supernatural development. The scripture declares, "Be ye transformed" (Romans 12:2 KJV).

We are to seek transformation.

"But we all, with unveiled face, beholding as in a mirror the glory of the Lord, are being transformed into the same image from glory to glory, just as by the Spirit of the Lord" (2 Corinthians 3:18 NKJV).

"And all of us, as with unveiled face, [because we] continued to behold [in the Word of God] as in a mirror the glory of the Lord, are constantly being transfigured into His very own image in ever increasing splendor and from one degree of glory to another; [for this comes] from the Lord [Who is] the Spirit" (2 Corinthians 3:18 AMP).

"Do not be conformed to this world (this age), [fashioned after and adapted to its external, superficial customs], but be transformed (changed) by the [entire] renewal of your mind [by its new ideals and its new attitude], so that you may prove [for yourselves] what is the good and acceptable and perfect will of God, even the thing which is good and acceptable and perfect [in His sight for you]" (Romans 12:2 AMP).

"Don't copy the behavior and customs of this world, but let God transform you into a new person by changing the way you think. Then you will learn to know God's will for you, which is good and pleasing and perfect" (Romans 12:2 NLT).

"So all of us who have had that veil removed can see and reflect the glory of the Lord. And the Lord—who is the Spirit—makes us more and more like him as we are changed into his glorious image" (2 Corinthians 3:18 NLT).

We are to begin our spiritual transformation now and not wait until we get to heaven.

The word *repent* means to "make a deliberate and willful decision to stop sinning; to make every effort to turn away from sin and live a life that is pleasing to God." It means that we are to set the direction on the compass of our minds on the path that leads to the kingdom of heaven and then follow the course laid out before us.

Heaven is our destination and should be our desire. Heaven is a place of beauty, holiness, and love, on a scale that ascends every realm we could possibly conceive. It is a marvelous domain that requires a fully transformed heart.

We must realize that we can seek the Lord Jesus Christ directly for His help in transforming our thought lives, our emotions, our feelings, and our hearts. Think of it—the most intelligent being throughout all of heaven and the universe can help us to understand and learn of a way of life that is superior in every way and form.

If we become diligent in seeking God, Jesus Christ, and the Holy Spirit for their help in transforming us into new persons, our thought processes and thinking abilities will soar beyond anything we could possibly imagine. We will be able to walk in a superior way of life.

Being diligent in seeking the Lord Jesus Christ for a transformation of our hearts will produce a way of life that is capable of overcoming every temptation and sin with ease. This is the beginning of a miraculous life, a victorious life of supernatural demonstration. To obtain the power to overcome sin is one of the first steps in living a life of superiority. There is no struggle. There is no laborious battle. There is only an instantaneous victory. These fiery darts of temptation just bounce off our shields of faith.

To live a powerful life, totally free from sin and any temptation, is just the beginning of walking in the power of the Holy Spirit. When we learn how to live free, then we will be able to set free. The power and skill of defense will lead to the demonstrations of a powerful offense. The basics for a powerful sin-free life begin with a transformed heart.

The transformed heart learns quickly how to shelter under the power of Jesus Christ and His blood. His blood is bursting with powerful energies of life—of supernatural life, of restoration life, of resurrection life. His blood provides us the ability to receive deliverance from sin. And Jesus's blood provides us the ability to maintain deliverance from sin.

The ability to receive and apply the blood of Jesus Christ in our daily lives is the cornerstone and foundation to experiencing the supernatural way of life that was meant to be from the very beginning of time.

Until we are well trained and spiritually developed, there will be many bumps in the road.

We need help to maintain our relationship with the Lord. If we are wounded or our spirits broken, then the best first-aid treatment is communion. Communion is a powerful tool for spiritual warfare.

If we are overwhelmed with sinful desires or ungodly dreams, thoughts, imaginations, or addictions, we must diligently seek God for His help to deliver us. With determination, we must seek Jesus and learn of the power of His blood and His body, that we may be able to live the kind of life that God meant for us to live. This is repentance.

To establish a pure relationship with God, as Adam and Eve once had, is God's goal for us. It is only possible through Jesus, His blood, and His body.

When we partake of communion, we are taking it for the purpose of receiving the Lord's help in getting rid of everything in our lives that is not pleasing to Him. That also includes any disease or sickness.

One gentleman I encountered shared that he was given a six-month death sentence. He had cancer.

He learned of the healing virtues that were available in communion and then made the decision to take communion on a daily basis. At the end of six months, the doctor gave him a cancer-free diagnosis.

Learning how to receive the miraculous virtues demonstrated in the communion prayer is an essential part of living the Christian life that we desire to have—that is, a fulfilled life of restoration in every area. Having the ability to provide restoration to our physical beings is wonderful, but keeping a clean wedding garment is just as important.

We take communion, first of all, to recognize Jesus as our loving high priest, that we may receive His work of restoration within us. We are able to not only receive physical restoration but also the restoration of our wedding garments, that they remain clean and spotless from any form of sin. We want to get rid of every sinful thing in our lives.

Through communion, Jesus will provide a purifying transformation of our desires and thoughts. If we have desires within our hearts that are not pleasing to Him, He can create within us new desires—desires of righteousness—that are pleasing to Him.

We can receive His help and intervention in our lives (especially through the practice of communion) to live that life of righteousness.

We must seek purity, and we must not try to justify any kind of lifestyle of sin. Sin will always be a hindrance, but this is one battleground that can be won. Taking communion is the best and most successful battle plan for overcoming every evil intent of the heart and securing a victorious life of righteousness.

"Therefore *do not let sin reign in your mortal body*, that you should obey it in its lusts. And do not present your members as instruments of unrighteousness to sin, but present yourselves to God as being alive from the dead, and your members as instruments of righteousness to God. For sin shall not have dominion over you, for you are not under law but under grace" (Romans 6:12–13 NKJV, emphasis added).

God has provided us with the ability and power to prohibit sin from taking over our lives. All we have to do is learn how to receive Him. Every time we fellowship with the Lord, we must open up to ourselves to receive Him, His instruction, His wisdom, and His transforming work of our hearts. We must run to Jesus—run to the one who has provided life eternal for us. He is the source of power that provides victory for every evil confrontation and is able to provide us with the supernatural power to cast down every evil desire.

"For if the blood of bulls and of goats, and the ashes of an heifer sprinkling the unclean, *sanctifieth to the purifying of the flesh: How much more shall the blood of Christ*, who through the eternal Spirit offered himself without spot to God, *purge your conscience* from dead works to serve the living God?" (Hebrews 9:13–14 KJV, emphasis added).

The Blood of Jesus Sanctifies

The blood of Jesus cleans, renews, and maintains our spiritual garments. The blood of Jesus will purge our consciences from all dead works. The blood of Jesus has the power to protect and purify our thoughts.

The Bottom Line

Only one thing that will provide sufficient provision for us in these last days and that is having an active relationship with Jesus Christ. Developing a relationship with the Lord Jesus Christ is the single most important achievement we can accomplish.

It is through this relationship that He will show us how to pray—for ourselves, for others, and for every situation we encounter. We must also realize that communion has no time limits. It can be a brief meditation, or it could turn into an amazing time of fellowship for an hour or two.

CHAPTER 13

THE COMMUNION PRAYER

PRAYER THREE

Jesus, I come before You and ask You to forgive me of my sins. Wash me clean with Your blood and make me as white as snow. I ask You to remove every spot and blemish from my mind, body, spirit, and soul. Remove from me every sin and any wrongful desire to sin. Create within me the desires that You desire for me to have.

Jesus, as You have forgiven me, so do I forgive those who have sinned against me. I release from my mental prison anyone who has hurt me in any way, and I ask You to forgive them, bless them, and help them spiritually. I forgive others as You have forgiven me, so that on the day of judgment, I will not be held accountable for the sin of unforgiveness.

Father, hide me under the shadow of Your wings of protection and safety, and cause my enemies to be at peace with me. Let now every curse spoken against me be broken.

I ask You to open my heart and fill it with Your presence. Create in me a clean heart, oh God. Renew a right spirit within me. Deliver me from sin, evil, and temptation. *Make me rapture-ready! Amen.*

TAKING THE BREAD AND THE FRUIT OF THE VINE

[Bless the bread.]

Bless now this bread that represents Your body.

I receive now this bread, Your body. I now receive your body of health, healing, and youthful rejuvenation. I receive this in Your name, Lord Jesus. So let it be. Amen.

[Take the bread.]

[Bless the fruit of the vine.]

Bless now this fruit of the vine that represents Your blood.

I receive now this fruit of the vine, Your blood of atonement. Make us one, of intimate and close relationship. Let Your blood of deliverance and resurrection life flow through my entire being. Let our hearts become one, united in the highest form of Your righteousness and love. I receive this in Your name, Lord Jesus. So let it be. Amen.

[Take the fruit of the vine.]

When we partake of communion, we should think of it as receiving a blood transfusion. His blood has all the antibodies necessary to destroy every evil infection that tries to weaken or destroy us. Sin is a deadly disease, but it can be destroyed.

This prayer will help us maintain a position of right standing with the Lord. It affirms our righteousness and allows us the ability to boldly approach God without fear.

Communion is not just for church. It is for us, and we can partake of it at home. I frequently partake of communion.

When I was shown how to write the communion prayer, three aspects needed to be emphasized with great concern; it is crucial for us to understand them.

1. It is important and urgent to maintain and keep a clean garment of righteousness.

2. It is very important to comprehend the absolute necessity to forgive—and that there are dire consequences to our very being if we don't.

3. The time has come that the bride must make herself ready for the bridegroom. And the only way we can make it in time is if we seek the Lord for His help in making us ready. That is why we must pray for ourselves, "Lord, make me rapture-ready."

CHAPTER 14

THREE PRAYERS OF NECESSITY

These three prayers—the prayer of protection, Psalm 91; the prayer of transformation, the Receptive Prayer of God's Character; and the prayer of restoration, the Communion Prayer—are essential and will provide every necessity for our survival in these last days. These three prayers cover protection, deliverance, provision, and personal transformation. Their purpose is to establish a secure future. Those who intercede for themselves now will set in motion a supernatural intervention for their future.

The wisest move any Christian can make is to prepare spiritually. Time to develop a deep personal relationship with the Lord is slipping away very quickly—and survival modes are now becoming necessary.

I was shown the three prayers that are essential for our protection and survival.

The prayer of protection, Psalm 91, covers miraculous intervention and protection. This includes protection for our physical, mental, emotional, and spiritual well-being. We are engaged in spiritual battle as well as a physical battle.

The prayer of transformation, Receptive Prayer of God's Character, is for the establishment of God's very character and nature within us. This prayer allows God to empower us to live like Him. This prayer will empower and provide direction in our prayer lives. The miraculous way of life will become prevalent. This prayer will enable us to walk in the supernatural realm and demonstrate the powers of heaven here on earth.

This is the purpose of the Receptive Prayer: "So all of us who have had that veil removed can see and reflect the glory of the Lord. And the Lord—who is the Spirit—makes us more and more like him as we are changed into his glorious image" (2 Corinthians 3:18 NLT).

The Communion Prayer is for healing and maintaining a pure and spotless wedding garment of righteousness. This prayer keeps us in a right-standing position with God. Communion is a prayer of restoration and healing. This prayer will not only keep our garments of righteousness clean and spotless, but it also will open wide a door for a pure relationship with God. God loves to dwell within a clean and pure heart.

This is the purpose of the Communion Prayer:

"Restore unto me the joy of thy salvation; and uphold me with thy free spirit. Then will I teach transgressors thy ways; and sinners shall be converted unto thee" (Psalm 51:12–13 KJV).

CHAPTER 15

PLACE YOURSELF ON TOP OF YOUR PRAYER LIST

When you pray, put yourself on top of your prayer list—this is a must. Though I was taught in my youth to place myself last in my prayer life, as an act of humility, the Lord showed me that this was indeed a big mistake and not according to His Word.

"*First* remove the plank from your own eye, and then you will see clearly to remove the speck from your brother's eye" (Matthew 7:5 NKJV, emphasis added).

If our hearts are not right with the Lord, then our prayer lives will not be right. We will not be able to see clearly the direction in which the Lord would have us pray. Instead, we will stumble around in ignorance, praying something that we think is appropriate. We need to have clear vision before we start praying for others. Many times we miss the mark when we do not pray for the root cause of a problem. And then we wonder why nothing happened. Many things need specific pinpointed prayer in order to get results. And the only way we can know what to pray is if we clearly receive direction from the Lord.

We must get our hearts right, and our prayer lives will become powerful. Remember, it is the pure in heart who see God with clear and unobstructed vision.

These prayers are short and simple. They will help prepare for what is coming before the seven-year tribulation, and they will become a very vital asset for those who dwell on earth during the seven-year tribulation.

- Leaving your first love
- Deception
- Fear
- Hatred
- Unforgiveness

These five things will destroy many Christians, and many Christians will fall away

The only way to survive these last days of great turmoil is to establish our hearts in the deepest love relationship with the Lord. We must protect ourselves from losing our love for God, being swallowed up in fear, becoming overwhelmed with hatred, or rejecting God's grace through deception. We need to start preparing and protecting our hearts right now.

"Guard your heart above all else, for it determines the course of your life" (Proverbs 4:23 NLT).

The heart is the very source of life's consequences. If our hearts are not right with the Lord, then our ways of life will not be right with the Lord. This is why we need transformed hearts. This is why we must seek the transforming of our hearts of Him. This is why we need to develop personal relationships with Him.

"Keep and guard your heart with all vigilance and above all that you guard, for out of it flow the springs of life" (Proverbs 4:23 AMP).

The command to "guard your heart" is essential. What we determine to pray for ourselves today will prepare the way for our ability to stand in the future. It is imperative that we do not delay in preparing ourselves through prayer. Everything we can do now will be of great benefit.

I strongly encourage you to start a daily prayer vigil for yourself. Pray these prayers daily and as much as possible.

Do not rely on emotions or feelings as to whether or not these prayers work. Rely on the end results as they manifest. Be diligent, persevering, and determined. These prayers can be said at any time of the day, and you do not have to limit yourself to once a day.

Praying effectively for yourself is the best way to secure yourself and position yourself for the rescue of others.

Do not fall into the imaginary trap that you are completely unmovable or unshakable. There is no one so spiritual that he or she cannot fall—*no one!* Your security depends upon your relationship with the Lord. Your spiritual state of being means nothing. No matter how strong you may think you are spiritually, without the Lord, you can easily fall flat on your face.

Everyone, even those who are spiritually mature, will face temptation and tribulation. Many will have the fortitude to remain stable because of their relationships with Lord. These will not fall or fail, though opportunity to fail will present itself. Those who strengthen their hearts with the presence of the Lord will have no desire to permit sin or temptation into their lives. They will be on their guard and will be able to discern every kind of deception. They will be successful in their ability to overcome during this time of persecution.

You must seek to be filled with the fullness of God. Do not allow yourself to be counted among the casualties.

CHAPTER 16

TIDAL WAVE OF EVIL

A powerful and *supernatural tidal wave of evil* is coming that will sweep over the whole earth in a most persuasive attempt to invade our thoughts, dreams, emotions, feelings, and flesh. Every ounce of preparation that we make for ourselves will increase our ability to resist this evil, but we have to start doing something now. We have to start praying for ourselves *now*.

As I was bringing this book to completion, the Lord prompted me to add two other prayers that will provide great benefit for our future. They are the Psalm 23 and Matthew 6:9–15, the Lord's Prayer.

CHAPTER 17

PRAYERS

PSALM 23

The Lord is my shepherd; I shall not want.

He maketh me to lie down in green pastures: he leadeth me beside the still waters.

He restoreth my soul: he leadeth me in the paths of righteousness for his name's sake.

Yea, though I walk through the valley of the shadow of death, I will fear no evil: for thou art with me; thy rod and thy staff they comfort me.

Thou preparest a table before me in the presence of mine enemies: thou anointest my head with oil; my cup runneth over.

Surely goodness and mercy shall follow me all the days of my life: and I will dwell in the house of the Lord forever. (KJV)

THE LORD'S PRAYER

In this manner, therefore, pray,

Our Father which art in heaven, Hallowed be thy name.

Thy kingdom come. Thy will be done in earth, as it is in heaven.

Give us this day our daily bread.

And forgive us our debts, as we forgive our debtors.

And lead us not into temptation, but deliver us from evil: For thine is the kingdom, and the power, and the glory, forever. Amen.

For if ye forgive men their trespasses, your heavenly Father will also forgive you:

But if ye forgive not men their trespasses, neither will your Father forgive your trespasses. (Matthew 6:9–15 KJV)

It is very important that we grasp the meaning of the very last portion of this prayer. We need to forgive sinners, no matter how ungodly they are. It is for this reason that we need a transformed heart. For without it, it will be almost impossible to produce forgiveness on our own. A heart of flesh will find it most difficult to forgive, but a supernaturally transformed heart produced by

God will find a way to forgive. This type of heart will have an ability to see and understand the reality of things as seen from the Lord's perspective, not ours.

These three prayers are the most important prayers we will ever pray. These are tremendous prayers of transformation, safety, and preservation, but it all begins with you.

You are the one who has to take the initiative to prepare your future.

Your future, your survival, and your security depends upon how you prepare yourself through prayer. Only a transformed heart will be able to see clearly the direction in which one should go. Only the pure in heart are able to see God. Those who have clear vision will know exactly what to do.

You cannot afford to procrastinate. Your way of life is about to change drastically in ways you cannot imagine. You must pursue God for a transformed heart. He can change it. He can open the eyes of your heart.

You have to pray daily. Just as you have to eat food on a daily basis, it is of absolute necessity that you spend time in prayer on a daily basis.

The Prayer of Protection

Psalm 91

He that dwelleth in the secret place of the most High shall abide under the shadow of the Almighty.

I will say of the Lord, He is my refuge and my fortress: my God; in him will I trust. surely he shall deliver thee from the snare of the fowler, and from the noisome pestilence.

He shall cover thee with his feathers, and under his wings shalt thou trust: his truth shall be thy shield and buckler.

Thou shalt not be afraid for the terror by night; nor for the arrow that flieth by day;

Nor for the pestilence that walketh in darkness; nor for the destruction that wasteth at noonday.

A thousand shall fall at thy side, and ten thousand at thy right hand; but it shall not come nigh thee.

Only with thine eyes shalt thou behold and see the reward of the wicked.

Because thou hast made the Lord, which is my refuge, even the most High, thy habitation;

There shall no evil befall thee, neither shall any plague come nigh thy dwelling.

For he shall give his angels charge over thee, to keep thee in all thy ways.

They shall bear thee up in their hands, lest thou dash thy foot against a stone.

Thou shalt tread upon the lion and adder: the young lion and the dragon shalt thou trample under feet.

Because he hath set his love upon me, therefore will I deliver him: I will set him on high, because he hath known my name.

He shall call upon me, and I will answer him: I will be with him in trouble; I will deliver him, and honour him.

With long life will I satisfy him, and shew him my salvation. (Psalm 91:1–16 KJV)

THE PRAYER OF TRANSFORMATION

Receptive Prayer of God's Character

Lord Jesus, I receive of You now the infilling of Your Spirit of love.

I receive of You now the infilling of Your Spirit of righteousness.

I receive of You now the infilling of Your Spirit of wisdom and revelation.

I receive of You now the infilling of Your Spirit of peace.

I receive of You now the infilling of Your Spirit of joy.

I receive You, Holy Spirit; fill me with Your presence.

I receive Your blood, Lord Jesus; fill me with Your blood.

In Your name, Lord Jesus, amen.

THE PRAYER OF RESTORATION

Communion Prayer

Jesus, I come before You and ask You to forgive me of my sins. Wash me clean with Your blood and make me as white as snow. I ask you to remove every spot and blemish from my mind, body, spirit, and soul. Create in me the desires that You desire for me to have.

Jesus, as You have forgiven me, so do I forgive those who have sinned against me. I release from my mental prison anyone who has hurt me in any way, and I ask You to forgive them, bless them, and help them spiritually. I forgive others as You have forgiven me, so that on the day of judgment, I will not be held accountable for the sin of unforgiveness.

Father, hide me under the shadow of Your wings of protection and safety. Cause my enemies to be at peace with me. Let now every curse spoken against me be broken.

I ask You to open my heart and fill it with Your presence. Create in me a clean heart, oh God. Renew a right spirit within me. Deliver me from sin, evil, and temptation. Make me rapture-ready. Amen.

Taking the Bread and the Cup

Bless now this bread that represents Your body, Lord Jesus.

I receive now this bread, Your body of health, healing, and youthful rejuvenation. I receive this in Your name, Lord Jesus. So let it be. Amen.

Bless now this fruit of the vine that represents Your blood, Lord Jesus

I receive now this fruit of the vine, Your blood of atonement. Make us one, of intimate and close relationship. Let Your blood of deliverance and resurrection life flow through my entire being. Let our hearts become one, united in the highest form of Your righteousness and love. I receive this in Your name, Lord Jesus. So let it be. Amen.

May the Lord bless you and keep you. May His love shine upon you. May you know Him in the fullness of His love.

—Robert North

Another Book to Consider

Another book you might consider reading is *I Am with You*, by my mother, Betty North.

I Am with You is a book of miraculous events, of the power of prayer, and of two special encounters she had with the Lord in heaven when she suffered not one but two cardiac arrests. During this time, she got a glimpse of heaven and had two wonderful encounters with Jesus. Her heart was broken when she was told she had to return, as there was more for her to do. She did not want to leave heaven. She desired more than anything to remain with Jesus.

At the age of eighty seven, she shares some of the most memorable miracles that have taken place in her life.

The power of prayer is real. Having a personal relationship with the Lord is real.

She simply wants everyone to know that the Lord can be a part of their lives, as it is with her.

I Am with You by Betty North

Printed in the United States
By Bookmasters